SOUND

OF

FALLING SNOW

Stories of Recovery from Autism
and
Related Conditions

EDITED BY ANNABEL STEHLI

B

BEAUFORT BOOKS

NEW YORK

IN AFFILIATION WITH THE GEORGIANA INSTITUTE

FIRST EDITION

ISBN 0-8253-0532-2

Published in the United States by Beaufort Books
in affiliation with
The Georgiana Institute
www,georgianainstitute.org

Distributed by Midpoint Trade Books
www.midpointtrade.com

2 4 6 8 10 9 7 5 3 1

PRINTED IN THE UNITED STATES OF AMERICA

FOR MARK AND SARAH STEHLI

CONTENTS

FOREWORD

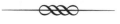

Jeff Bradstreet, M.D.

When Annabel Stehli contacted me about her most recent book, *Sound of Falling Snow*, I was immediately intrigued by the title. Her past glimpses into the mysterious world of autism had helped me understand my own son's sensory challenges. Over the years, Annabel has become a friend and ally in my quest to bring relief to children with autism, Attention Deficit/Hyperactivity Disorder (ADHD), and sensory integration disorders. Perhaps the most telling story of our shared challenges to educate our colleagues about auditory processing disorders and the ways we help with it comes from our visit to a nationally syndicated pediatrics television program.

We were barely introduced when the pediatrician-host asked, "So, if auditory therapy is so helpful for children with autism, why does the American Academy of Pediatrics (AAP) claim there is no evidence to support its benefits?"

I suppose that was a fair question from the uniformed outsiders' perspective, but it also begged the bigger question, "How could the AAP miss the abundance of supportive data published, ranging from physician-authored medical textbooks to peer-reviewed publications?" Certainly, we had gotten past the "no evidence" point of the evaluation by now.

And to my thinking, we have. Auditory therapy in its many forms is practiced by hundreds of credible clinicians. Thousands of children have been helped with simple, low-risk interventions that stimulate the auditory cortex with sounds and music. Clinically, we know music and sounds have profound impacts on feelings. Every movie director depends on music to set the mood. We all feel it. Music can brighten a cloudy day and calm a savage beast.

But the modern application of digitally enhanced music can do much more. Auditory therapy enhances the level of neurotransmitters in many areas critical to communication, receptive language, and cognition. Music has even been documented to stop status epilepticus, the worst form of epilepsy.

My interest in auditory therapies and digital auditory training extends from my professional roll as a physician with hundreds of patients with autism-related disorders to my paternal role as the father of a now nine-year-old boy with autism. Our first experience with auditory integration training (AIT) came after reading Annabel's first two books on the subject. My wife and I took our son to an experienced practitioner when he had just turned five. At that point, he was afraid of playgrounds. We would sadly watch as other children gleefully climbed through the tubes at McDonald's while Matthew would only sit in the ball pit, wiggling around and keeping his distance from other children. Every time we tried to force him into a tube slide, he would panic. Halfway through his first ten-day auditory training session, we took him to the beach for a break. There was a playground with the dreaded tube slides. He ran for the playground and climbed up the ladder for the tube. My wife and I watched in amazement as he climbed into the tube and emerged smiling at the bottom. After repeating this several times, he ran over to another child, grabbed him by the hand, and led him over to the slide to go down together. We were shocked.

I suppose the scientific purest might dismiss this as an uncontrolled anecdote. But is that true? I actually believe it is a carefully observed study of one child. And with enough $(N = 1)$ studies, clinicians gain practical experience and shape the true art of medicine, therapy, and clinical practice.

As I think about *Sound of Falling Snow*, I recall an ice-cold night spent in at a ski lodge in Canada. It must have been nearly three in the morning when cold air creeping into my pajamas woke me up. My blanket had fallen off and I needed to get warm. I sat in front of the gas fireplace in the living room and gazed out at moonlit, snow-covered mountain peaks. After finding the warmth I needed, the beauty of the evening drew me out to the balcony overlooking the valley below. Clouds moved in quickly from an approaching front and the moon disappeared, to be replaced by tiny snowflakes. It was well below freezing, and the snow was crisp and hard. With no other sounds that evening, I could actually hear the tiny flakes make a barely audible tinking sound as they hit the metal roof and blew against the glass behind me.

Annabel told me I needed auditory therapy the first time she met me. It is true that crickets bug me — quite literally. I cannot think if they are chirping outside my study window. I may have hyperacousis (the medical term for overly sensitive hearing). But then without it I probably wouldn't hear those important heart murmurs and I would likely have never experienced the sound of falling snow firsthand.

Sometimes our children with learning disorders and autism are so sensitive to sounds that they cannot function normally in a world full of painful noise and distortion. They avoid people (noisemakers) and withdraw into the safety of self-stimulating play. I doubt the view that autistic behaviors are meaningless. After years of living with a hyperacoustic child with autism, it is obvious the behaviors are meant to help them cope with a world where sensory input exceeds their abilities to manage the stimulation. Ears, after all, process more information than any other sensory system we have.

I think sensory dysfunction represents a serious, perhaps foundational issue for children with autism and related disorders. Auditory therapy represents a key tool for therapists and families in the battle to overcome the sensory wars being waged in nearly every classroom and too many living rooms.

— Palm Bay, Florida

ACKNOWLEDGMENTS

Joan Mathews, professional editor, writer, network parent, and close friend, took on the final edit of this book without hesitation, performing the task graciously, expertly, and fast. This on top of having been the fourth and final editor of my first book, *Sound of a Miracle*, and contributing not only a chapter on her son, James Williams, but the index for the second, *Dancing in the Rain*. Amazing James, in addition to giving us the only story written by a recovered child, was of inestimable help in the production of the book. His computer expertise is unparalleled in my experience although he is only fifteen (and the author of five novels). Thank you so very much, Joan and James.

The mothers who have allowed their children's case histories to come to light in this book deserve the highest praise. When you have a child in recovery, it is easy to forget the challenges of the past, to go forward thanking God and rejoicing in your newly normal life without looking back. Not only have these exemplary parents been willing to submit their stories, they are also willing to stand behind them and be there for those who need information, direction, and support. Although in some cases pseudonyms have been used, the authors may be contacted through the Georgiana Institute, www.georgianainstitute.org.

I would especially like to thank Eric Kampmann. Eric is my publisher and member of the Board of Directors of the Georgiana Institute. When, at a low point in the winter of 2002, I was considering devoting the rest of my life to writing fiction and kayaking the white waters of the world, he inspired me to keep the Institute going, complete *Sound of Falling Snow*, and be up for another round of publicity. Without Eric this book would not have happened.

If it takes a village to raise a child, it takes a community to launch a new treatment modality. I wish to thank the donors to the Georgiana Institute over the years, my immediate and extended family, especially my aunts Pat Haines and Jane Coverly, my friends, network parents and auditory training practitioners, and the Board of Directors of the Georgiana Institute, all of whom have provided me with the emotional and financial support needed to keep promoting AIT. Most especially, I would like to thank Charles K. Wynn, Jr., who steadily inspired and encouraged me when I wanted to say "enough already" and be done with it.

All of these people can be proud of the fact that, according to Bernard Rimland, Ph.D., Director of the Autism Research Institute, "Autism now bears the potential for recovery." Special thanks to you, Bernie. You started this whole thing when you called me up in 1988 and said, "I hear you *claim* to have a child who has recovered from autism." When I bristled, challenging you to call Magda Campbell, the psychiatrist who had originally diag-nosed my daughter Georgie's autism, and she said, "Why, yes,

Georgie was indeed severely autistic," you offered to do research if I would write the book, and that was the beginning. You gave AIT credibility.

I would like to thank Keith McBurnie. When the FDA forbade the importation of the original French equipment in 1993, it was Keith who had the guts, vision, and perseverance to find a way, and in 1998, Digital Auditory Aerobics, American-made and faithful to the protocol, was *exempted from scrutiny* by the FDA and could be legally described as an educational intervention for the purpose of remediating impairments in auditory discrimination. Bravo, Keith. Without you, where would we be?

Finally, I would like to express my profoundest gratitude to Guy Bérard, M.D., inventor of AIT.

INTRODUCTION

"Certain noises, projected at the right pitch, can incapacitate even a stone-deaf terrorist; the bones in your head are brutalized by a tone's full effect, whether you're clutching the sides of your skull in agony or not," wrote Marshall Sella in "The Sound of Things to Come," an article on Elwood Norris in the *New York Times Sunday Magazine*, March 23, 2003. Elwood Norris, founder and President of American Technology Corporation in San Diego, has developed High Intensity Directed Acoustics (HIDA) — sound as a weapon. When I read the article, I thought of a young autistic man I know who once spent a good part of his day walking around in a circle, holding his head and keening. Using a method that allows the non-verbal to communicate, he claimed that auditory integration training (AIT), the therapy that is the main subject of this book, had taken away the sound of the buzz saw in his brain, rescuing him from a lifetime of intolerable noise.

A six-year-old boy diagnosed with autism and since recov-

ered, commented on the results of his ten days of Auditory
Integration Training, where he had listened to filtered and modulated music for two half-hour sessions each day. "I can still hear
people blink but I can tune it out," he said. Imagine hearing people blink, and then imagine needing to tune it out. If you can hear
people blink, imagine the auditory onslaught of louder sounds.
"Get me out of this noisy world!" No wonder autistic people are
in their own world. No wonder learning disabled children day-
dream as much as they do.

A dyslexic botanist once said to me, "I never go out in the
woods to collect specimens when snow is forecast. I can't stand the
sound of it." When I challenged him, saying that this was unusual, that most people can't hear snow falling, he said, "What's the
matter with you? Are you deaf?" and stormed away. He didn't like
the idea of being different, and refused to believe he was. He did-
n't want to think his hearing was hyperacute and distorted and that
this was related to his dyslexia. That it could be treated was not
something I was about to suggest. Had he been a three year old
with distorted speech or no speech at all, and I had seen him clap
his hands over his ears when a faucet was turned on, I might have
been unable to resist the impulse to slip his mother a copy of one
my books, *Sound of a Miracle* or *Dancing in the Rain.*

Guy Bérard, M.D., retired otolaryngologist, developed AIT,
treating thousands of cases of *La Dyslexie* over four decades of
practice in Annecy, France. In the French vernacular, *La Dyslexie*
covers a broad spectrum of leaning disabilities involving reading
and communication problems. Some of these cases, including my
autistic daughter's history, are described in his book, *Hearing Equals
Behavior.* I have him to thank for the quality of my daughter's "nor-
mal-range-functioning" life today. Ever since she was treated by
Dr. Bérard in 1977, achieving the impossible by recovering to

become, as she puts it, an *oxymoron* (she likes puns, and she's good, isn't she?), I have been beating the drum for AIT.

AIT has been researched (see www.georgianainstitute.org for a summary of research studies), is sometimes covered by insurance, and is generally available within an hour's drive of most people in the U.S. Digital Auditory Aerobics, based on the Bérard Method of AIT, has been "exempted from scrutiny" by the FDA since 1998. I can legally say that AIT often remediates impairments in auditory discrimination sometimes associated with disorders such as autism, pervasive developmental delay (PDD), attention deficit disorder (ADD), attention deficit/hyperactivity disorder (ADHD), central auditory processing disorder (CAPD), dyslexia, and related disorders. And I can whisper the outrageous, that autistic toddlers diagnosed with hyperacute hearing who receive AIT are mainstreaming into kindergarten four years later with no label and no support.

I hope that, if you find your child in a story in this book, you will investigate the possibility that his behavior and ability to learn may be affected by his hearing.

Annabel Stehli
The Georgiana Institute, Inc.
georgianainstitute@snet.net
www.georgianainstitute.org
June 2004

Sound

of

Falling Snow

Mark

———— ⦁⦁⦁ ————

Pam Pritchard

A MOTHER'S STORY

My six-month-old baby boy looked just like the baby in the detergent ads as he played peek-a-boo with me from his crib.

As he approached his first birthday, people remarked that he looked like an angel child. It's true. Mark had an ethereal quality about him and was healthy in every respect. I couldn't get enough of him, and I recall a joking remark: "If you kiss that baby any more, you'll kiss his skin off." He was a joy. My one year old began to crawl to the newspaper on the floor, point, and look expectantly at me until I read the paper to him. When he could speak in sentences, he phonetically read the newspaper to me, not to mention reading from the *Physicians' Desk Reference (PDR)* in his pediatrician's office. The doctor gaped in amazement and proudly called in every doctor in the building to witness and applaud the remarkable event. How cute, I thought. I was twenty years old and did not know the word *hyperlexia*, much less the word *autism*.

As Mark continued to develop "on time" according to Dr. Spock, I could not help but notice that at age two, the famous "No!" year, he had never uttered either the word "no," or the word "yes." If he didn't want spinach he would say, "Take it off, the spinach," and when I would say, "Do you want a cookie?' he would echo, "You want a cookie!" His meaning was clear — he did not eat the spinach, and he got the cookie. Nevertheless, unusual patterns were emerging.

He became consumed with love for the NBC peacock and, in lieu of a teddy bear, slept with a disintegrating piece of a matchbook cover bearing a picture of the beloved peacock. He could recite verbatim Walter Cronkite's introduction to the nightly news. Friends and family thought it was adorable and applauded his intelligence. I began to wish he would just say *yes, no, I want . . .,* or *Give me the . . .* It was many years before I heard those words.

By age three, Mark's attention wandered, his eye contact was intermittent and easily diverted, and he spent long periods of time off on his own. Never did I hear the interminable questions of a three year old, "Why is the grass green?" and "Where is my toy?" Never a, "What are you doing, Mommy?" It made for much easier child care, and I should have known then something was amiss. I especially should have known when we visited a friend and her three year old. I saw my son reach out and act as if he wanted to play with the little girl. He had never approached another child before, and I remember it made me cry. The tantrums began then, too, but it's difficult to distinguish between a three year old's "I want my way" tantrums and the nervous-system overload tantrums of the autistic child. I was young, a first-time mother, and an only child. What did I know of typical child development? Looking back on it, the only tools I had were love, tenacity, good instincts, and an unshakable belief — born perhaps of naiveté — that my son would be okay. Armed with those intangibles, I embarked with my boy on our decade's long journey of diagnoses, special education, therapies, judgment, rejection, triumphs, and above all, trial and error.

Around this time Mark had his annual check-up with our pediatrician (of the *PDR* reading incident), who told me that he had "noticed for some time that something was wrong with the child." Wondering why he hadn't mentioned it before, I dutifully took my child to the psychiatrist he recommended. My husband, from whom I was now separated, also had a private appointment with the psychiatrist, as did I. She gave me her conclusions: The father is narcissistic and the boy has childhood schizophrenia. I was never told the contents of the file on me. I suspect it read something like *Mater Frigidus*. No suggestions were made as to what could be done.

THE PATTERNS BROADEN

At age four, my son entered a typical nursery school, staffed with lovely, caring people, especially one of the helpers who happened to be a "little person." When the mothers picked up the children, all the kids ran to them squealing, "Mommy, Mommy, see what I drew today!" All but one. My son was cradled contentedly by the side of the loving little woman and happily came with me when I took his hand. During group songs at school, Mark stood looking at the corner, making a high-pitched sound all his own. I observed this and was amazed — things like this were not happening at home. Within a few months, he was gently, but firmly, expelled from nursery school. At that moment, I learned two important things that would stay with me throughout the journey: I. My son was decidedly not "typical," and I had to face it and do something about it; and 2. There is a "people factor" that is paramount in working with a special needs child. People — not "placement" — make all the difference. Over the years, certain adults have been magic with him whereas others, despite the best of credentials and intentions, were not. Still others were downright harmful. I can still see the little nursery school helper lovingly keeping my son close to her. I wish she could see the man he has grown up to be.

LIFE AT HOME

Home was always easier than school and the outside world. The trial and error method applied to home life too. For example, the less eye contact Mark made, the more we played a game called "follow Mommy's eyes." The less *related* he wanted to be, the more games we played. With endless patience, my mother rolled a rubber ball back and forth with him and never quit when he wanted to wander off. You get the idea. Instinct on the part of all who loved this delightful child led us to ways of keeping him interacting with us. I only wish we had done more. Had I known this was *the* thing to do to help him, we would have stayed in his face every waking moment.

Progress appeared slowly, but it was visible and by the time Mark was four, we became acclimated to living with the difficulties, which continued to include a high frustration level, tantrums, and only peripheral involvement with the other children. To balance the equation, there was the occasional "gotcha" moment. Jill, a neighborhood playmate, who had been accurately termed by my mother "the bad seed," delighted in hollering to my son through the mail slot, and when he, time and again, fell for her ploy, she reached in and pulled his hair. One day my mother, God bless her, a more aggressive sort than I, took my son's place on the inside of the mail slot and when Jill did her thing, my mother gave Jill's hair a good yank. Yeah, Mom!

SPECIAL EDUCATION BEGINS

We found a special nursery school when Mark was four that was comprised of children with a spectrum of difficulties. The school worked mostly with behavior modification, rewards, and time-outs (about the only modality available at that time). Everyone on the staff lived up to my "people factor" criterion. I recall Mark's enormous difficulty putting on his jacket by himself. With patience and consistency such as I had never before seen, the teachers worked with him, teaching him step by step how he could encode in his brain the process of "jacket donning." It took the better part of a year, but, by gum, he was no longer "the boy who couldn't put on his jacket." I learned an invaluable lesson about patience and repetition, which I incorporated into everything we did at home. I was more than happy with his progress at this school, and best of all, my son was happy there.

One Tuesday, I was told that on Wednesday my son was to be at school promptly at noon because a Doctor Connor or O'Connor (I didn't write it down) was to evaluate him. As fate would have it, on my way to school with our carpool child, the little girl lost her lunch in the back seat. I was delayed. The school director was in a snit because I was late for *The Doctor*, whom I now deduced must be a VIP.

After my son had been evaluated by Dr. Leo Kanner, I was called in to speak with the doctor. A kind, grandfatherly man, he sat me down and told me he had no doubt that my son had what was known as autism, a word new to me. He gave me a brief clinical explanation of autism, little of which I retained, and finished by stating, (and with all due respect to Dr. Kanner, this is close to an exact quote), "Unfortunately, autistic children never develop normally. Your son will never be able to function on his own in society. I recommend that you immediately place him in a setting that can care for him properly." At least I was listening closely enough to know what the word "setting" meant.

Operating on pure instinct, I replied instantly and emphatically, "I understand, but no. I'll find another way." Those were the only words I was able to get out at that moment. Dr. Kanner remained sympathetic, told me he thought I was making a grave mistake, and offered no further suggestions. I never again saw or spoke with the legendary Dr. Kanner, the man who coined the term autism in the 1940s, but many years later I did learn who he was.

THE DIAGNOSIS GETS LOST

Between the Kanner meeting and our next school, no one called my son autistic. They wrote down a lot of things on various evaluations and school reports (childhood schizophrenia, emotionally disturbed, behavior problem — whatever came to mind). In my heart, I rejected all of those labels, and thus was not very focused on diagnoses. It was a very long time before autism resurfaced in my son's life.

OUR "OTHER WAY" JOURNEY BEGINS

Trial and error next led to a neurologist, who was a good man and somewhat helpful. After my son hopped on one leg for the doctor, he prescribed a little-known drug called Deaner, which actually calmed and focused him. Then he was switched to ritalin, which, as we know is an upper, which frequently has a calming effect on hyperactive children. Frequently, but not always. My precious four year old was so high on the amphetamine, he literally dashed about the house for eight or ten hours, his little tongue occasionally darting in and out of his mouth. I could do nothing but watch him and wait. It was one of the worst days of my life, and my son's life, I'm sure. Although Deaner was good, it was soon to be "banned" for my son, which in retrospect I regret. If there is a drug that truly helps, and doesn't hurt much, I say, use it. Unfortunately, along the journey, we were given very little opportunity to explore this maxim.

At age five, after extensive searching and insurance company battles, Mark was enrolled in a day-school kindergarten, which was part of an excellent private psychiatric facility (which permitted only the medications its doctors deemed appropriate — so much for Deaner). The principal and teachers were great and more than lived up to my "people factor" expectations. They, too, utilized behavior modification, and despite their candy-giving rewards (Why would anyone give sugar to hyperactive children??!!), my son began to interact with the others and he liked the school. At home, I tried diet to calm him down — high protein, no processed sugar, etc. — pretty progressive for its time. It worked well, except the school candy threw things off. Trial and error. Terrific things happened for my son during this time. He engaged in genuine play at home and school and loved his Tonka trucks and racing car track. All nice, typical five-year-old stuff. He was excited about the school's parents' day for three weeks prior to that event, and on the big day, came running to me and my parents, showing us his classroom, and offering us refreshments. Progress — real progress!!

The psychiatric facility at the school was an eye-opener for me. My five year old had weekly appointments with his psychiatrist, and I had weekly appointments with mine, as well as my meetings with the social worker. At my first shrink appointment, a doctor with a slight smile (which he sustained for a whole hour) looked deeply into my eyes and asked what it was I thought had caused my son's condition. I babbled things like "I have no idea" and "nothing unusual ever happened," but the doctor just kept staring and smiling at me — waiting for the *real* answer. After a three or four minute stare, I recall how much I wanted to say, "Come to think of it, maybe it was the time I locked him in the closet with the snakes." No matter how much the psychiatrists believed I had "caused" this condition, I and my instinct knew better.

My son was not the only one who learned a lot from this school. For one thing, I learned that traditional psychiatry with five year olds with autism does not work. One day, my social worker informed me that my son, amid much crying, had told his doctor, "We had a bird and it died. And then we got another bird and it died, too." It was obvious, she said, that he was dealing with feelings of loss in his life and questioned me about what was happening at home. The fact of the matter is that we had indeed bought two parakeets that died within one month. Not good for the parakeets, but I confess I very much enjoyed telling the social worker about it, although I was never certain she believed me.

On the plus side, I got a new social worker — an incredible woman who treated me not as a suspect but as a mother dealing with life. She offered practical mothering suggestions when I was at my wit's end and personally counseled me when life was confusing. She was my confidant and advisor and I loved her. She, in turn, liked me and adored my son. She and her husband became "adoptive grandparents," inviting my son to their home for weekends with them and their teenagers, and later to their summer home in Arkansas. The family became lifelong friends to me and to my son. They were the poster children for the "people factor" in action.

A major milestone for me was the time I was called to a huge meeting — doctors, administrators, teachers, outside consultants.

I had no idea who most of them were. They explained to me that my son's "condition" was known to be caused by mothers who were "distant" with their children. They said, ever so gently, that they knew, of course, that I loved my child and had the best intentions, but that unknowingly I had not related to him enough, touched him enough, played with him enough. Often, they told me, such mothers are clinical, intellectual, and uncomfortable with touching and playing with their children. They could not have described me more inaccurately. I made only one comment at that meeting. I asked, "If that is true, why doesn't this happen to every child in an orphanage or to all children in dire poverty whose mothers have no time for them?" The professionals smiled, mostly at one another, and did not respond. My instinct and I knew they were dead wrong. I did not qualify. I was the mother who had been at risk of "kissing the baby's skin off," and no one would have described me as intellectual, clinical, or distant. I was and still am a live-by-your-guts, touchy-feely kinda gal. I breathed an internal sigh, but I knew enough not to mess with a good thing. I had learned the psychiatry game early on, and played along for the next three years. It was a good school. My son was happy there.

MAINSTREAM WAS UPSTREAM FOR US

By age five, the little guy had already been IQ tested. Despite hyperactivity and inattention to the test, he scored 155. Because he was highly verbal and, clearly, very very intelligent, the problem could not possibly be autism, said the professionals. And then one day, the decision makers decided that this child was so intelligent, so verbal, and doing so well — it was time to "mainstream" him into public school. The head teacher fought the decision tooth and nail, and I resisted as well, but to no avail. So, at age seven, off Mark went into third grade in the regular public school. The school principal, a highly revered educator and definitely a "people factor" guy, met with us and I gained confidence that, under his guidance, we'd be okay. However, the gentleman fell ill and retired during the summer. We were now in public third grade without a rudder. Simply stated, it was a disaster. The progress of the previous three years slowly began to dissipate. I took him to a world-famous clinic, where I was told, "We've observed your interaction with your son and we think you handle him too well." To this day, I have no idea what that meant.

One parents' night, in a classroom full of parents crunched into child desks, the teacher walked over to me and announced authoritatively, "Mrs. Pritchard, your son is an emotional cripple." I'm not a vindictive person by nature, but in his case, I made an exception. Then the new principal, a pleasant but clueless woman, stopped me in the hall one day and explained that she "cannot have my son making such a fuss in the corridor because we have workmen here doing renovations." That did it! I announced he would be leaving the school and I set about finding a new school for him. After all, I was pushing thirty by this time and beginning to get the hang of this. Mainstreaming (a fairly new concept then) became a dirty word to me, and it was quite some time before I would entertain the idea again.

ANOTHER EXCELLENT SCHOOL

I guess we were lucky, if you can call it that. Mark enrolled in a special ed school that was part of the public system. For a year and half, Mark made more progress. The school had good teachers, caring people, and innovative programs. Mark even rode the bus to school and had a crush on a little girl named Lisa, about whom I teased him endlessly.

It goes without saying that there were difficulties. There

were, in fact, major difficulties. Tantrums in a seven year old are not as acceptable as they are in a two year old. The tantrums were our biggest problem and my son and I were both devastated by many, many instances of judgment and recrimination by other parents, people in the mall — in fact, by all of the unenlightened. I sometimes had a knee-jerk anger reaction to the outbursts. Many of the kids teased him cruelly and took unspeakable advantage of him; memories that he retains to this day. I prefer, however, to dwell more on the progress than the problems. We went bowling and shopping on Saturdays and to church on Sundays, Mark played with the other kids, had a next-door friend, and made random phone calls with his pal, asking people if they had Prince Edward in the can and if their refrigerator was running. By age nine, Mark could stay with babysitters and went to summer day camp, where he won a trophy for most improved camper. My little boy was growing up, doing basic kid stuff, albeit with his unique obstacles to overcome. And overcome he did.

WE MOVE AND HE MOVES ON

We moved to a new state, and my son underwent a slow but sure change from "special" child into semi-typical preteen and teenager. Again, I found an excellent school, where the "special ed" was part of the whole school and the teacher was a saint. That's the formula! He began to have the occasional friend, was more than capable of staying home alone for a couple of hours till I got home from work, flew by himself to Florida for long visits with my parents, and sang with the class in the spring pageant hosted by Harry Reasoner — an event he talked about for some time. I knew, and he knew, that life was harder for him than for the other kids. He struggled with taunting and rejection. Only as an adult did he tell me how much he hated being on the "special ed" bus and the other kids calling it the "retard bus." The mornings at school went well, but every afternoon, his concentration wandered, and he was tested for every possible cause. I learned years later from my son himself that the chalkboard had looked like a whirlpool to him as the afternoon sunbeams hit it, and he became lost in the vision. He had and still has visual and other sensory perception so different from ours, we can't even conceive of how life looks to him and how distracting it must be. There are many, many parts of his life (even now) that I'll never really know about — how did it feel to not know exactly how to look at or talk to the other kids no matter how hard you tried? How did it feel to be twelve years old, smarter than all the other kids (and even some of the teachers), and still it wasn't enough? How did it feel to be different? I could never really know. I still don't know.

THE TEEN YEARS

They were not your "typical" preteen and teen years in many respects, but there Mark was, out in the world tackling adolescence on his own terms. He did not drive or stay out late with friends — the usual parental worries. But he started listening to the current pop music and developed at least a passing interest in dressing in "cool" clothes, not to mention more than a passing interest in the typical (if not always totally appropriate) crushes on girls.

As far as schooling goes — you're expecting a "Then one day . . ." aren't you? Here it is. In moving from one town to the next, I misunderstood the rules, and our new town had no "special ed" for him. Off he went to public high school — definitely a bright and functional youngster, but totally unprepared for a huge public high school — almost as unprepared as the school was for him. A major meeting of the school administration was hastily convened to organize what I later learned was an Individualized Education

Plan (IEP), part of the law mandating that every child have an appropriate education. I was over thirty by then, and knew a lot, but I was still not totally on to the entire system. Several placement suggestions were made, most of them boarding schools, which my son and I visited. One private boarding school, in particular, was appealing. A pastoral, oceanside village setting an hour from home, with good teachers, beautiful acreage, a stream on the property — a real country club. Prep school for the "difficult to otherwise place." I decided to send Mark there, and thus began the next adventure on the big education journey. Here's how it went:

Mark made friends, brought his roommate home on weekends and went to his roomate's for weekends, and was dealing and interacting with the other boys, whom he referred to by names like Tank, Quacky, and the Pillsbury Doughboy. He was just plain growing up. It was all pretty good stuff until the school's owner returned from sabbatical to regain the reins, and things went downhill.

Early one afternoon, I got a call at work from my now fifteen year old, calling from HOME!! He had run away from school after a frustration incident, a primary reason he had been placed there. The headmaster (emphasis on the "master") went ballistic and screamed at him, "Get out! Get out of my school!!" So he did. To my eternal relief, when he ran away from school, he ran to his *own home*. Among this young man's shining qualities is that he can take a punch — heaven knows he's had enough of them in his life. He never shied away from going to school no matter how tough it got, so I trusted him and knew that he must have had good reason for running from this place. A school employee, incidentally, phoned me around 7 P.M. that evening, all atwitter because they had just noticed he was missing.

I had a talk with my son that neither of us will ever forget.

I urged him to go back and stick it out for six weeks until the holiday break. If, then, he still wanted to leave the school, I promised him I would officially remove him. There was a chance it would blow over, but mostly, I wanted him to leave on his own power and not be labeled as "the kid who ran away." That's exactly what happened. Six weeks later Mark said he wanted out, and I made the arrangements. Traumatic? Very much so, for both of us, but what I remember most is that I knew then and there I was dealing with a young person of character and integrity, whom I not only loved but respected enormously. The trust between us was forever solidified that winter. At the beginning of that new year, we had no school, but we definitely had one another.

A REALLY GOOD HIGH SCHOOL

Following six months of Band-Aid schooling measures (part attendance at the same old public high school and part home tutoring), we moved to yet another town. Coincidentally, a friend told me about a school across the street from our new house, a very small private school with eight or ten kids per class, consisting mostly of ex-tough kids, dropouts who were dropping back in. By now I was a tiger with the bureaucracy, and easily obtained funding from the school district, which said he wouldn't last there longer than a week. I met with the director, who is, I believe, the winner of my Lifetime Achievement Award for Excellence in the People Factor Category. It was an odd combination of my son and a school full of street-smart teenagers — sort of *Grease* meets *Revenge of the Nerds*. But it worked, and worked extremely well! Graduation ceremonies were held at a local banquet hall; and at the end they played Bette Midler's "The Rose." *"Just Remember in the winter far beneath the bitter snow lies the seed that, with the sun's love, in the Spring becomes the Rose."* Mark had blossomed and was never again to be just a seedling in waiting. I clearly recall stepping out of myself for a minute as I saw my son accepting his diploma, and beaming with joy, thinking, "Hey, look at us now!" I believe in reveling in the juicy moments in life — it balances out the distasteful ones.

COLLEGE (WOW!)

The high school director whom I adored then outdid himself and talked to his friend, an admissions director at a local university. They knew all about Mark's history but said, "Definitely yes, we very much want this young man at our school." That September, the "boy who couldn't put on his jacket" went off to college — with a jacket on.

The college experience was a quantum leap forward for him. Although it was only an hour from home, I arranged for Mark to rent a room off-campus. He took to college life like a duck to water. A fraternity approached him, but alas, rejected his application because he was not yet eighteen or, possibly, because he was a little different — not the rush chairman type. The landlord turned out to be a neat freak, and my son is anything but. Despite these minor setbacks, he was the happiest I had ever seen him. Academically, of course, he was exceptional, as a result of which he was sent to audit a weekly course at Yale. Another truly caring person, a Yale administrative director, popped into our lives and recruited him to do his junior and senior years at Yale with, I might add, close to total scholarship and grant funding (a financial necessity for me at that time). Can you believe it? His confidence level soared, and he got into his own groove at Yale. At home, he still had a hard time when his team did not win the televised football game. So we stopped watching sports. Predictably, some of the residence hall mates sniffed out the "different one" and pulled horrible pranks on him, but he prevailed. His first girl-

friend came along, he grew a beard in his attempt at latter-day
Berkeley nonconformism, and followed the Grateful Dead wherever possible. To this day, he is extremely proud of his Yale degree,
and rightfully so. One day in May, he was awarded a cum laude
diploma amid the ivy-covered buildings, and I don't even need to
tell you what a day that was for both of us.

POST-UNIVERSITY — LOOKING FOR HIS NICHE

Niche-finding is not easy for any recent graduate. It is consider-
ably more difficult for a young man with autism, and even more
difficult when the young man in question does not even know he
has anything with a name. He only knew that life in the working
world is tough. These years marked a bit of a dip for him — college had been much more his cup of tea. Despite my pleading that
he go to graduate school, Mark was eager to get out and seek his
fortune on his own.

Did I mention he is also adventurous by nature and fiercely
independent? He found himself in some great locations along the
way. San Francisco came first, but jobs in Silicon Valley did not.
He had the talent, but he didn't "fit." As you might imagine, the
job interview process as we know it in corporate America does not
allow for one with social and interactive difficulties and poor eye
contact. In the job search, he took rejection after rejection, and in
desperation, the Yale graduate took a job with the Postal Service.
Suffice it to say, employment on the night shift at a busy city post
office, sorting mail and having to coordinate quickly and hop to
the commands of the Post Office foreman, is not the place for a
young man with autism. Then again, we didn't know he had
autism, did we? He only knew that he felt like a failure, and the
confidence level of the college years began to recede.

Chicago came next. Our wonderful friend, who had been my

social worker early on, opened the door for a job with a computer consulting company there. The company quickly realized that their new employee was not cut out to consult and schmooze with the clients, but he did a great job manning the mainframe equipment from headquarters. He made decent money and, to the mother's delight, he had his Chicago adoptive family for support. But he hated Chicago. It was cold; he never made friends; and he became pretty depressed with the whole situation.

Change of location — that's the ticket! At least, that was my Mark's motto. So he sought and accepted a very good-paying job via a telephone recruiter whom he never met. It was in New Orleans. Gotta hand it to him — he chooses interesting places to live. He truly loved New Orleans — it's laid back, nonconformist, and without snow. He had a lovely, large apartment in an old house where he could hear the streetcar clang. He was making excellent money, getting involved in political causes, going to Mardi Gras and Jazz Fest, and best of all, friends began to appear — offbeat characters with names like John, The Tamale Man and Velvet, the hot New Orleans mama with a brood of children and her part-time husband, the cop.

Ironically, it was just at this time that I happened upon a Larry King interview with Annabel and Georgie Stehli. As they spoke of Georgie's autism and her trip back from it, major bells rang for me. I phoned my son and told him I thought everyone had been wrong all along since he was five years old and that he did indeed still have autism. He resisted at first, but after reading *Sound of a Miracle*, he grudgingly agreed that it may be so. As it turned out, it was just a short time later than he embraced the autism diagnosis as a partial explanation for the things that were happening to him.

Once again, life had thrown Mark another curve — in fact,

several nasty curves in a row. He was terminated from the job because he "behaved strangely" in the workplace. Although he remained in New Orleans for two years with no job (did I also mention that frugality is big with him?), it did not go well. Friends began to disappear or move away, and his activity-filled life gave way to too much isolation. Even his litter of feral kittens died in his closet. He was hanging on for dear life to one very special friend and her young child, and when she announced she was leaving the city, it was too much. He overreacted, to say the least — just too much for one person all at once. I don't know if he would agree, but I saw this as the low point of his life.

So, at the age of twenty-nine, as many of us have grudgingly done, Mark came home to Mother to regroup.

THE CLIMB BACK, THE ONGOING STRUGGLE, AND SUBSEQUENT SUCCESSES

Then came several months of living with Mom in a one bedroom apartment, anger and embarrassment at not having "made it," and weekly counseling sessions. Not the high point of Mark's life, but a breeding ground for his rise from the ashes. I, too, was not a happy girl during this period. As close as my son and I are, we don't make good roommates — especially in close quarters when he is beset with anger and frustration. I've tried to imagine being in his shoes at that time and am amazed at how we got through that period. Mark's made of stern stuff. Having recently "rediscovered" his autism and being at the low point in life's progress both came at him at once, but he didn't give up.

One bright spot was the auditory integration training (AIT) he underwent during this period. He spoke about how the music sounded and felt. A familiar song like Gordon Lightfoot's "The Wreck of the Edmund Fitzgerald" was transmuted into an atonal, avant-garde type of piece one might hear in a drafty "performance space" in Brooklyn. He also said in his unique, eloquent manner, that he felt "a relaxation of the force field around him." Mostly I recall overhearing him say that after AIT he felt a lessening of the constant feeling that he was being chased by a tiger. That was the first time I had any idea that he had the "fight or flight" response constantly coloring every experience. I can only imagine what that must feel like — always being chased by a tiger!! He said it so matter-of-factly — it had been part of his reality all along. AIT did help to slow down the tiger, for which we were both thankful. It's a lot more difficult, though, to pursue therapies with a strong willed thirty year old than with a young, dependent child. If only AIT had been available to us when Mark was younger . . . if only, if only. I could fill a book with "If only's," but I refuse to go there. We have so much else to focus on — the saga of Mark's successes, past, present, and yet to be found.

He did indeed climb out of that hole to move on to a succession of his own apartments, later into New York City, and currently into a lovely little apartment and a rewarding job in Hawaii, working as a coordinator with a disabilities-related agency. In his recent adult years, he does things that the books tell us autistic people can't do. I was gleeful when I learned he could dissemble a bit and tell a little white lie occasionally. He continues to amaze me sometimes with his observations of other's motivations, and he can often read me like a book. On the practical side of life, he's still underemployed and gets frustrated easily. He is anxious about not having yet achieved all he wants to do. He's brilliant, creative, and has that "I want to be somebody" drive. While his name may or may not end up a household word, those who know him well already think he's definitely "somebody."

I think Mark's story in a nutshell is best summed up by the

man himself. The details don't matter that much. This job and that job; his personal relationships and/or, at times, lack thereof. What matters is how he, himself, views his journey.

A SON'S LIFE SUMMARY: IN HIS OWN WORDS

Because I wasn't behaving "according to the book," that is, manifesting mental retardation as well as autism, I was, in effect, defined out of disability. This being the 1970s, the profession tended to hang trendy, but not terribly useful, labels such as "emotionally disturbed" on me. Later, through my teens and twenties, my identity was that of "weird computer geek."

I managed to compile a decent record in college, socially as well as academically. Delegate to Student Government, a brief stint as English Club president, and a regular at the Thursday night story readings and bull sessions. Tellingly, though, the only people who welcomed me into the dining hall when I got to Yale were two students from Hawaii.

It was not until the appearance of Annabel Stehli's *Sound of a Miracle* that it all started to click: the patterns in the veins of an autumn leaf, the ripples in the pond, and so forth. There was, indeed, something more to me than the merely weird or geeky. At last, it started to dawn on me how I had managed to find myself alone in the middle of a huge college mixer, a massive anti-nuke demonstration, and even a Grateful Dead concert!

Also, it explained why so many potential employers, who were intrigued by the resume of a Yale grad with computer skills, seemed so disappointed to discover that it belonged to me. I bounced around from job to job, finally ending up working for Yale itself in its renowned autism clinic. Since then I have spent most of my career in the fields of psychiatry and disability. I have even spoken to groups of several hundred at autism conferences.

Is this a "success story in autism"? That depends on what the meaning of the word "success" is. I have a tendency to measure myself not against other people with autism, but against other members of my Yale graduating class, many of whom are doing things like writing for network television, working for political campaigns, or in the case of Jodie Foster, piling up Academy Awards. The irony is that some say Bill Gates himself exhibits the traits of autism, which begs the question, why is he the world's richest man while I'm a cubicle rat? Then again, one might ask why I live independently and hold a professional job, while so many other people with autism, including many with a college education, languish at home or even in a "setting" such as a group home. Yes, I suppose this is, after all, a "success story" in autism.

FINAL WORDS: FROM THE MOTHER

I never thought undue modesty was one of Mark's traits, but he only touched on his years of speaking engagements and neglected to mention how good he is at it. He was, and still is, a sought after speaker at local, national, and international conferences on autism and related topics. I've seen him hold an audience of 300 people spellbound, after the doctor/researcher speakers had all but put the crowd to sleep. When he speaks to groups about his story, he is fond of saying, "When I was four, Leo Kanner told my mother to put me in an institution. She did — Yale!" A bit oversimplified, but it says a lot.

When I, from time to time, speak to parents of children with autism, I remind them that "in our day," there was almost no help. Even today, there is precious little assistance of any kind for the high-functioning adult with autism. With all the advances and choices of therapies, I remind parents of my number one concept: people make all the difference. Number two, in my opinion, is keep the child focused and interacting at all costs. Coming in at number three would be: expect a lot — you may not get it, but expect it. Beyond that, a little luck and a lot of faith help.

The success story isn't over. Mark continues on his very own journey, but don't we all? My son is a gifted writer, a genuine wit, intelligent and knowledgeable and conversant about almost everything, and has a social conscience. He's good company, fun to be with, and in general, a good and decent person. That's not just his mother's opinion — ask anyone who has had the pleasure of knowing him. True, Mark's life is not where he'd like it to be and he still has some overcoming to do. Again, don't we all? I still nag a bit (although time and distance have slowed me down a lot), and as I've always done, I expect a lot from him — perhaps more than he expects from himself. He is a bit "eccentric" and sees himself as a tiny bit "different," with what he calls a "low sociability quotient." Well, many say things like that about Einstein.

Perhaps the next time you encounter someone on a bus or interviewing with you for a job — someone who seems just a bit off plumb, but you can't put your finger on it, please think twice. Autism doesn't always show, but it's there and, best of all, there are success stories within autism. I always believed my son would be okay, and he is. Adults who have dealt with autism are light-years ahead of those of us who have never had to overcome anything remotely like it. My son is one of those who have overcome and will always continue to do so. He is very, very, very okay.

MATTHEW

———— ∞∞∞ ————

Linda Seiford

GUIDED BY GOD

On a blustery Thursday evening in March, I took my beautiful, nine-year-old son to our Catholic church for a healing Mass. As we sat and listened, I held tightly to Matthew's hand. I felt as if I were watching a movie of our lives together. Every memory and all of the feelings I had experienced over the past nine years came flooding back; I lived through them all again. Every joy, every fear, every worry, and every doubt was part of an enormous tangle of emotion wrapped in love.

After the sermon, we slowly progressed to the front of the church for our blessing. When it was our turn, the priest asked what it was we were seeking from God. All of my emotion was released in that instant, and through my many tears, I asked Him to heal my son. I couldn't elaborate. I was too emotional. But I knew God would understand. As we left the church that evening, I knew things would change, but I had no idea how.

Less than one week later, I took my son to the pediatric dentist for a routine check-up. After his cleaning, they called me in for the actual examination. Because of his history of extreme oral defensiveness, I was thrilled to see how relaxed he was and to learn how well he had done to that point. I was so proud of him! I was on cloud nine! But a few very short moments later my cloud disappeared beneath me. I came crashing down to earth when the dentist told me that my son had a tumor. In that instant my life stopped. I heard him tell me all of the pertinent information; everything you'd expect to hear. But I couldn't breathe. I couldn't understand. I had prayed for my child to be healed, and now I was being told he had a tumor. It couldn't be. It made no sense. Why would God do this? In an instant, my life had changed. All of a sudden, nothing else mattered. I couldn't believe that we'd struggled so much to get this far just to have it end now. Nine years was not enough time. And yet the next two weeks, while waiting for surgery, seemed like an eternity.

I once heard that God is working on our lives from above, much as a crafter works on needlepoint. From the underside, the needlepoint appears to be an incredible tangle of strings; a mess. Yet, from above, the pattern displayed is beautiful. God sees the pattern; He knows the plan. We only see the mess. I wanted to see from His vantage point. This made no sense. This was not Matthew's destiny.

Matthew has the most beautiful blue eyes. They look like kaleidoscopes, and they're magical. They can transport you to a place of peace even when you're not anywhere near there. I certainly wasn't. Yet over the next two weeks, I looked into those beautiful blue eyes and took the kaleidoscopic tours. I went back in time and remembered every last second of our lives together.

From the moment that my seven pound six ounce baby boy was born, I knew that he was special. Not just the specialness that every mother feels for her child, but special in the sense that Matthew seemed to be able to perceive things others couldn't. I learned very early on that he could sense what I was feeling often before I could identify the feelings. I trusted his perception and reaction to others knowing that he could sometimes "see" things I couldn't. I knew enough then to know that his gift would need to be protected from others, and more importantly, he from his gift. But at the hospital, with him in my arms, I did as every mother since the beginning of time has done. I counted fingers and toes, I marveled at the creation in my arms, and I made promises of unconditional love to my child. He was a perfectly healthy baby boy, and God had given him to me. I felt overwhelming love, and I knew that together we could do anything. I anticipated a normal life together. I expected the attainment of developmental milestones. I looked forward to the exchange of stories with other parents. I hoped for a long, happy, and healthy life for my son. I had no idea what was in store.

Because Matthew was my first child, I had no basis for comparison. But I believed he was developing as he should. He had some quirky behaviors, but nothing I considered to be truly worrisome. He didn't require much sleep as an infant, but neither did I as an adult. His day began long before the sun rose, but mine prior to his birth, ended long after sunset. I knew as a seasoned insomniac that circadian rhythms aren't always changeable, and so we adapted.

In many ways, Matthew was quite advanced. At a very young age his emotional intelligence was greatly developed, his thought process more complex, and early speech, at times, quite precocious. Flags, however, were raised when he didn't repeat the things he said. Long before he could crawl, I heard him say, "Mama, Mama. I love Mama." It would be years before I would hear him say that again. My apprehension also increased when he didn't crawl at an age appropriate time. He was of average size when born, and he quickly grew to be a very healthy and round little cherub. He was content to sit and study the world. If something was out of his reach, he wouldn't expend the energy to go to it, he'd find a way to bring it to him. While secretly pleased by his inventiveness, I was concerned and felt a little like a failure. I worried that I hadn't exposed him to something that would enable him to learn to crawl. I believed it was my fault. As a result, I spent a great deal of time demonstrating the crawling motion, and trying to coax him to do the same. I looked quite ridiculous. Matthew was very amused by my antics, but he wouldn't crawl.

At fifteen months of age, for no apparent reason, he decided it was time. He crawled of his own accord. He didn't rock back and forth. He didn't go around in circles. He didn't fall over. From initiation, he was expert. It was as if he'd been practicing mentally for months, but didn't want to do it until he knew he would be successful. Having perfectionistic tendencies myself, I worried about this possibility, and did my best to reinforce the idea that life is to be experienced and not perfected.

The relief I felt when Matthew achieved this milestone was relatively short-lived. By fifteen months of age, most children are walking. My angel had just started to crawl. I voiced concern to his pediatrician. While he acknowledged my concern and expressed several possibilities, he reminded me that Matthew was still in the normal range for walking development. Because Matthew was continuing to progress, we decided to wait until he was eighteen months old. I did my best to remain positive, hoping and praying that everything would work itself out.

Much as he did with crawling, Matthew studied others, and their modes of ambulation. He, however, was content to either crawl or walk on his knees. This made absolutely no sense to me. It was as if he weren't aware that he had legs and feet beneath his knees. We walked together holding hands, but if left to his own devices, he would drop to his knees and walk on them. Again, he and I practiced. Hand in hand, we walked for miles each day in an attempt to strengthen his little legs. We also spent a great deal of time doing walking exercises. I sat leaning against the bookshelf in the bedroom less than one foot away from him. He was propped up against the bed. My goal was to get him to take even one step alone. Every once in a while, he was able to do that. Then he'd quickly fall into my arms. With every attempt, I created a huge scene complete with all of the fanfare you'd expect from a mother cheering on her little one. The confusing thing about it, however, was that he didn't seem to be able to repeat the motion. He didn't seem to connect the body sensation and/or directive with the movement. To add to my confusion was the fact that he could walk independently when watching himself in a mirror, but couldn't do it otherwise.

At eighteen months, of his own volition, he walked independently. I was stunned and ecstatic! He continued to walk on his feet from that day forward. My relief was palpable. That, to me, had been the critical milestone. He had achieved it, and I felt that as a result my worries had ended. When we took Matthew to his pediatrician two weeks later, I entered the office the proudest parent there. I didn't have a care in the world. My baby was walking independently, and that, to me, meant he was fine. In hindsight, I entered that office much as a lamb going to slaughter; completely unprepared for what was to come.

As I watched my baby walk down the hallway for the

pediatrician, I was elated. The pediatrician, however, wasn't. He was concerned with Matthew's gait. He mentioned things like cerebral palsy, and other deteriorating muscle disorders. He also suggested we pursue evaluations from specialists. In one instant, my perfect life had gone from one of proud mommy to terrified and uninformed parent. My world was rapidly becoming one that would be comprised of examinations and evaluations. My baby's fate was unknown. This was the day we entered hell.

While other children were playing with blocks, my child was visiting neurologists, geneticists, physical therapists, occupational therapists, and speech therapists. While other children were playing in the sandbox, my baby was being observed for any and all abnormalities. While other children were being cradled and rocked to sleep, my little boy was being held down for blood draw after blood draw. This continued for months over the Thanksgiving and Christmas holidays. While other families were celebrating, we were living a nightmare.

Having to hold your child down for a blood draw is one of the worst things for a parent to endure. Every time we'd go in, Matthew's little eyes would cling to mine filling with tears, pain, and questions I couldn't answer. And after every round of tests were completed, we were given no answers. There seemed to be no explanation for the difficulties Matthew was experiencing; difficulties that were becoming more pronounced as he aged. Speech was very difficult for him. We'd heard words and some phrases in the past that we'd never heard again. He'd talk in his sleep, but could not talk while awake. He could mutter to himself while playing, but while interacting with others, he couldn't seem to repeat or speak intelligibly. Words were not clear or purposeful, and he was becoming more frustrated with every passing day. He knew something was wrong. He knew his body wasn't cooperating with his

mind, and his eyes frequently filled with tears. I would kneel before
him, take his little face in my hands and say, "Mattie, Mommy will
find the answers for you. You have to believe in yourself. Someday
you'll be able to say anything you want. I promise."

The medical community was offering no answers. It felt as if
they were approaching the testing at that point with a hit-or-miss
attitude. Matthew was continuing to make progress, but things
were difficult for him. We weren't about to subject him to increas-
ingly invasive testing with no promise of an answer. Thus, we put
a hold on any further testing. His pediatrician supported this decision. It was clear to me then that I would need to be instrumental
in finding the answers to help my son. It was then that I began my
nightly ritual of research after I'd put him to bed. It was then that
I realized that I wasn't the cause of his difficulties, but that I could
be instrumental in his progress. It was then that I began the fight
for my child. I knew he was trapped in his own little body. I also
knew that it would be up to me to help set him free.

Night after night, my search yielded nothing. Night after
night, I was left feeling that my son was losing precious time.
Night after night, I prayed. One evening I was driving home alone
and because it was dark, I felt confident that no one would see me.
So, I pulled into a parking lot and cried. At that point my prayers
changed. I prayed not for my baby, but for me. "Please help me to
help my son," I prayed. "I don't know how to help him. Please help
me." That evening was a turning point. While researching, I stumbled onto the Apraxia-Kids Web site. I read and printed as much
information as I could find. As the printer turned out page after
page of information, I wept. Not everything sounded like my son,
but enough so that I knew that I was finally on the right track. In
the wee hours of the morning, I walked into our bedroom, turned
on the light, shook my husband to wake him, and handed him the

growing stack of papers saying, "Read this. I've found our baby."
We read and cried together. Elated to finally have some answers
and a direction to help our son. This literally was an answer to my
prayers.

During that same period, I contacted our local school district
to perform assessments on Matthew, hoping that they could also
shed some light. It was through these wonderful people that I first
learned of sensory integration dysfunction, another profound factor affecting Matthew. So, at the ripe old age of three, I enrolled
my child in Early Childhood Special Education (ECSE). It hurt
me to know that I'd be separated from him so much, and that I
couldn't provide the special help that he needed. I worried about
strangers, and the care that he would receive. Would he be okay?
He was essentially nonverbal. How would I know if something
were wrong? But I knew that I had to let go for him to get the help
that he needed, and over the next several years we met some of the
most special people I've ever encountered. With the help of special
education teachers, occupational therapists, physical therapists,
speech therapists, assistants, aides, family, and friends, Matthew
started to blossom. I saw purposeful activity, and life in his eyes.
Together we learned sign language. I learned how to reach him,
and how to help him organize. I learned how to give him what he
needed. They helped me to reach a part of my baby that I hadn't
been able to reach before, and I will be forever indebted to them.

For a time, things progressed smoothly. Matthew was making good progress, but change to our status quo was necessary.
Matthew was making the transition from ECSE to kindergarten in
the fall and needed to be reassessed. We discussed the types of
tests to be conducted, and the adaptations to be made that would
allow him to perform to his potential. After several weeks of testing, we received the evaluation from the school psychologist. I was

devastated by what she had written. In her report, she stated that she classified Matthew as being severely mentally impaired with an IQ of less than 50. I knew this wasn't true, but I also knew the damage that this could cause if others viewed him this way. I didn't want him to give up on himself. My husband and I debated this issue with the school psychologist during an Individualized Education Plan (IEP) meeting, and requested that he not be assigned that label. IQ scores are considered to be extremely unfair to apraxic children, and it is difficult to assess their true knowledge. Given the fact that Matthew had only been speaking for a short time and his vocabulary was extremely limited, there was no way that he could adequately express himself to achieve a reliable IQ score. He needed time. I felt as if Matthew's fate were hanging by a thread. Thankfully, another professional at the meeting offered us an alternative. At that time in the state of Minnesota, a child was not required until age seven to have any label other than the blanket ECSE label in order to receive special services. She suggested we keep the blanket label until that time. A consensus was reached, and I knew that if nothing else, this would buy him the critical time that he needed.

During his kindergarten year, Matthew flourished. He not only had excellent support, but he had a wonderful special education teacher. I volunteered in her classroom, and tried to learn from her. I questioned her about anything and everything that I felt could be helpful to Matthew. At that time, I also questioned her about central auditory processing disorder (CAPD). I wanted to know if she believed CAPD could be a contributing factor to Matthew's difficulty. She wasn't certain, but she thought it could be a possibility. She supported me in my research, and she tried to help. She saw glimpses of what we saw in Matthew, and there was enough doubt in her mind to give him the time he needed to develop. She supported our decision to maintain an ECSE label until age seven, and she helped us find a new program/school for him for the following year. I was so grateful to her for her help, and for the genuine love and concern that she showed to all of the kids in her charge.

The next year for Matthew was very difficult. By Christmas, my happy and eager to please little boy cried when he had to go to school. He'd never done that before. On the days that I volunteered in his classrooms, he cried when I had to leave. I knew something was wrong, so I began questioning others. As if in answer, I began to overhear comments made in front of the special education children. Comments such as, "Our kids don't have those books. I guess it's because they're so far beyond what they can do."

After Matthew's seventh birthday, his special education teacher confronted me about reevaluating him. She emphatically stated that we were out of compliance with the law because his birthday had passed. She stated he needed a new label immediately. I informed her that we were having him tested privately by the university. We had decided to have him evaluated by both the neuropsychology and audiology departments. His special education teacher requested that I discuss the testing with the school psychologist. In an attempt to comply, I went to see the school psychologist. It was my intent to answer any questions he might have, and to inform him that the testing was in progress. Our brief encounter did not go as I had planned.

As I began to discuss the psychological testing to be conducted and the testing for CAPD, his pleasant demeanor changed. His response to me was that I shouldn't "waste" his time. Because he had attended a conference where CAPD was briefly discussed, he apparently felt qualified to discourage me. His response to me was, "They only test children with average IQ scores, and that isn't what I'm hearing about your child." He had never even seen my child. I walked out of his office, ignored his "advice," and pursued the testing for my son. The results confirmed that he has an auditory processing disorder. And despite his difficulties, he was found to be a gifted visual learner with an average IQ. In a very short time, Matthew had gone from testing in the severely mentally impaired range to testing in the average range with giftedness. I could only imagine what he would truly be capable of if we could identify all of his needs, get him the appropriate help, and then test him again. He was not severely mentally impaired. This was quite a different diagnosis than that which the school psychologists wanted to give him; the difference of a life — his life.

At that time, I began looking into other options for Matthew's education. My son's spirit was failing. His gift of perception was contributing to its demise, and I couldn't allow that to happen. While I don't believe he was privy to all of the negative comments being made, he certainly felt the sentiment. This became glaringly apparent when he told me "they don't think I can do anything." At that point, I asked Matthew to be my brave big boy, and I asked him if he would complete what remained of the school year. He told me he would finish the final two months. I marveled at his strength, and told him that he wouldn't have to return the following year.

A short time before, I had seen an announcement in the paper for an informational meeting on homeschooling. I knew instantly that this was what Matthew needed. I attended the meeting, did further research, conducted interviews, and then made the decision to pursue this option. True to his word, Matthew completed the school year. Several months later as we began our school year, I knew we'd made the right decision. On our first day, I was sitting on the ground. Matthew kneeled behind me, gave me a big hug, and said, "thank you for doing this for me." We've never looked back. He has his love for learning back, he's doing well academically, he believes in himself, and he, once again, is the happy child he deserves to be.

During the Christmas season of 2000, I felt the need for more guidance. I had never stopped my nightly rituals of research, but none of the information I had been finding seemed quite right. Again I prayed. "Please help me to help my son. I'm missing something. He needs me to help him. Please show me how." One evening while shopping in a local bookstore, I felt compelled to browse the special needs section. I stumbled across *Sound of a Miracle* by Annabel Stehli. I could tell from the cover that this book was about an autistic child. I knew Matthew was not autistic. Yet, something told me I needed to read the book. I stood trying to reason with myself for several minutes. This was, after all, the holiday season. My Catholic guilt told me I should be buying for others and not for myself. Yet, I couldn't dismiss the feeling. I purchased the book and devoured every word in it within twenty-four hours. It was a powerful and moving story.

I was so moved, in fact, that I contacted the the Georgiana Institute, the foundation started by the author and her husband. I wasn't sure why I was calling, but I felt I needed to do so. I expected the phone to be answered by a receptionist, and I expected the phone call to yield nothing. What I experienced, however, was quite different. Peter Stehli, Annabel's husband, answered the phone. We had a wonderful conversation; it was powerful. In fact, I hung up the phone, sat shaking on the floor, and wept. My youngest son came to me very concerned. He hugged me and asked me what was wrong. I explained that my tears were happy tears and that I'd finally found someone who could help his brother. He smiled, hugged me and said, "Oh, Mommy. I love you so much." We remained crouched on the kitchen floor, embracing and motionless for about five minutes. I knew this was another turning point.

In my conversation with Peter Stehli, I learned that a conference was being held three months later in Connecticut: "A Celebration of Breakthroughs II." I couldn't believe it! I felt so lucky to have learned about this, and to have the opportunity to attend. Three months later, for the very first time I left the boys home with their daddy, and accompanied by my mom, I flew half a country away in search of help. In my heart, I knew that I was finally going to find some answers. I also knew that the same treatment that had helped the Stehli's daughter would help my son.

I arrived at the conference early the first morning completely prepared to soak up as much information as I could. I attentively sat through every session, and I took as many notes as I could; notes I still reference. I intended to pick every brain there. Resultantly, long after the sessions had ended, I conversed into the very early hours of the morning with many people who were kind enough to share their knowledge and experience with me. The conference was phenomenal! In two days' time, I had more questions answered than had been answered in several years' time. But just as important as the information I acquired were the incredible people I met. Their stories completely recharged me, and honestly, they gave me a new way to look at things. I no longer felt alone. For in that conference room, there were hundreds of people who knew exactly how I felt; many of whom were paving the way for my son and me. I am so grateful to all those who have gone before us, who remember what it was like, and try to pass on all of the knowledge they've gained in an attempt to make our lives easier.

While at the conference, I called home frequently. One evening, I excitedly discussed all of the information I had been taking in. It was at that time that I told my husband that I believed Matthew should go through auditory integration training (AIT), and that we should get a golden retriever therapy dog. He was stunned, but agreed to both wholeheartedly. In hindsight, these were two of the best decisions we have ever made. Liberty was born in October 2001. We had to wait for her, but she was well worth the wait. If any dog were to have wings, she would. She has the kindest soul, and she always seems to know what is needed. She has helped Matthew immensely. She has helped all of us. She really is our best friend; our angel.

When I returned from the conference, I learned that there were no AIT practitioners in the state of Minnesota. Therefore, Matthew and I made the trek to Wisconsin for ten days of AIT in the summer of 2001. Of course I hoped that this would be the "magic bullet" for him, but I also knew that there were no guarantees. AIT did, however, prove to be very helpful for Matthew and the changes were noticeable the first day. His sensory defensiveness decreased, his attention and eye contact improved, he became toilet trained, and his vocabulary increased. The biggest change, however, seemed to be with cognition. Concepts that had been so difficult suddenly seemed to make sense to him. His thought process seemed to encompass a broader range, and he understood the relationship between behavior and consequence. It was incredible!

Though we had been able to obtain the treatment in a neighboring state, I knew that not all families would have that option. I wanted to make the treatment available for them. So, in 2002, I returned to Connecticut to pursue the training necessary to become an AIT practitioner.

I continued with my research looking for other pieces to fit into Matthew's puzzle. After his first round of AIT, I learned of a special needs symposium to be held in February 2002. I made arrangements to attend. Again, I was being guided. The dynamics of the group literally held me captive. I felt as if I were on the verge of a major discovery, but wasn't sure what it was. I learned an incredible amount of useful information, and repeatedly heard reference to a place called Camp Avanti. After the symposium, I was unsuccessful at all attempts to obtain information about the camp. But somewhere in the deep recesses of my mind, I remembered a past coworker whose son had attended a special needs camp. On impulse, I contacted her. She confirmed that her son had attended Camp Avanti, and she gave me all of the necessary information. At the same time, she warned me that there was always a waiting list, and that positions had been filled since the previous summer. I wasn't deterred. While I knew the chances of getting my son in were slim, I needed to try. When I made the call, I was informed that all spots were, in fact, filled. However, my son was put on a waiting list.

In May 2002, I wrote an article that was published in our church newspaper entitled "A Special Child . . . A Special Blessing." I was facilitating a support group for parents and grandparents of children with special needs, and wrote the article in an attempt to reach those who needed the help. I truly believe that this article helped to get my son into Camp Avanti, because shortly thereafter, I received the call that he was in. I was thrilled! My intent in writing the article had been to help others, but in some way, I feel it helped us too.

Camp Avanti is a place that provides an intensive occupational therapy program for children aged seven to twelve who have learning and/or sensorimotor disabilities. It is located in Hudson, Wisconsin, and is a fantastic place! I knew it was what Matthew needed! While there, he participated in therapeutic riding, swimming, kayaking, music, arts and crafts, sailing, outdoor activities, and other therapies for sensory integration. The changes we saw, and continue to see, brought tears to our eyes. Matthew became much more independent and social. He took more initiative and he seemed happier. He was in the perfect environment for him; he fit in beautifully. For once, he wasn't the "different" child, and this gave him the confidence he needed to allow his magnificence to shine. Everyone understood his challenges, and not only were they equipped to handle all of his needs, but they were able to teach him ways to meet his own needs for integration and organization. I'm so thankful that he was able to get in, and that he'll be able to return for the next several summers.

Because Matthew did so well in the therapeutic riding program at Camp Avanti, I began searching for a similar riding program for him to participate in outside of camp. Much to my dismay, all of the organizations I contacted had waiting lists; some over one year long. I discussed the subject with my uncle one day, and he became so excited. He knew of a program just beginning, and he was immediately on the phone getting the information for me. A few short weeks later, my sons and I were regular visitors at Agape Acres in Rosemount, Minnesota. Not only did Matthew participate in therapeutic riding there, but my youngest son and I also took riding lessons. We spent several days every week riding, cleaning stalls, brushing horses, and making friends. It did wonders for all of us. Matthew has always been very appreciative and loving toward me, but after so many years of uncertainty, research, therapies, and battles with insurance companies, I felt very weary. The people we met there loved my children, and they encouraged me in such a way that I once again believed we could conquer anything. I knew that I could press on, and I knew that Matthew would be okay.

With the guidance of our riding instructor and now very

dear friend, we purchased a beautiful and calm horse of our own. Her name is Ebony. I love to watch my children ride her. Matthew, who used to have difficulty with balance, now independently rides a 1,200-pound animal bareback. My son, who used to be terrified of animals, even small dogs, now snuggles right in to Ebony's perfect form. My Matthew, who perceived others' lack of confidence in his abilities, now exudes confidence of his own. The pride and happiness I see on his face is priceless.

In the fall of 2002, I decided to put Matthew through AIT again with me as the practitioner. Again I saw big changes. This time, however, the changes I observed in Matthew were focused in the areas of independence, sequencing, speech, and processing. All areas improved, and he achieved measurable growth in each.

While searching for answers and researching treatments to help my son, I've learned of many alternatives. Because of this, I'm grateful to have all of the notes I took at "A Celebration of Breakthroughs II" to help me make informed decisions. It is impossible to pursue all avenues at once. Thus, we address one issue at a time; we take it one day at a time. In October 2002, I was ready to tackle Matthew's diet. He had had traditional allergy testing in the past, but had only reacted to a couple of things that were easily avoidable. Over time, however, I had become aware of a deterioration of behavior and speech production after his consumption of certain foods. When we returned to the allergist to test for the ingredients of those foods, no reaction was observed. It was at that time that I started to question food sensitivities, and delayed food reactions. Once again, I returned to my notes. I knew I needed assistance with this, and thus, sought out a Defeat Autism Now! (DAN!) practitioner in Minnesota, knowing that he could order the appropriate tests to answer the questions I had.

The results of the tests confirmed what I suspected.

Matthew had intestinal dysbiosis, leaky gut syndrome, delayed food allergies to many common foods, and a yeast overgrowth. On November 1, 2002, we began a gluten-free, casein-free (GFCF) diet. He also began taking supplements to encourage the growth of good bacteria in his system, to kill off the bad bacteria, and to assist in the healing of his gut. The benefit of this approach was quite evident early on. Matthew's problematic eczema became nearly nonexistent, nasal mucosa decreased dramatically, body temperature normalized (was no longer hot and sweaty while sleeping), transition to sleep cycle improved, geographic tongue dissipated, sequencing improved, bowel movements normalized, skin color improved, attention increased, and oral defensiveness decreased. The phrase "you are what you eat" holds specific significance in this instance. In Matthew's case, what he was eating was keeping him from being who he is. I'm very glad we were able to make sense of this connection now.

While tucking my children into bed one evening, we were discussing education and the fact that I will be a doctor of educational and developmental psychology in the near future. Matthew turned to me and said, "We need to help the other kids like me." Through tears of pride, I promised him that we would. Through my teaching, writing, public speaking, and AIT, I make every effort to reach out and help all that I can. I've shared many tears with children, parents, and grandparents alike. I know what it feels like. I know the pain, the fear, the uncertainty, and the helplessness. But I also know the blessings. I've been chosen, and very blessed. All those with special needs children have. Never will I view the world in the same way. None of us will. Never will I take for granted a spoken word, a single step, a hug, or eye contact. Life holds new meaning; a greater purpose.

So where does this leave us? Do we have all of the answers?

No, but we're getting there. There are many things we still find confusing, and frustrating; many things we don't understand. But we're working on it. We're doing the best we can to find the answers without losing sight of how far we've come, and how we've gotten this far. We've been guided. It's all part of the plan. We're a part of God's needlework that is contributing to what will be a spectacular design.

As I sat in the hospital waiting room reliving memories and waiting for word from the surgeon, a realization hit me. While everything from the past seemed so traumatic, it seemed trivial by comparison with what Matthew was going through now. I had prayed for my child to be healed, and I had questioned God's plan. But suddenly it made sense. What Matthew had gone through before wasn't life threatening, but this could be. What he had gone through before was not what I would have chosen for him, but I do not understand the plan. It was then that I realized that my son has been fine all along. He doesn't need to be healed, and he doesn't need me to fix him. In fact, he's been fixing me. I've become so much more than I ever would have become without my son. His challenges have forced me to develop to my full potential so that I can help him achieve all that he can in this life. He needs to live out his life's purpose, but perhaps that purpose isn't to live life as others think he should. Perhaps his life's purpose is greater than we can comprehend with our limited intelligence. Perhaps his life's purpose is to help others to develop, and to truly understand how precious and special all of life is.

As I contemplated this, I saw the surgeon walking toward me. For an instant, I panicked. But from somewhere far off, I once again felt the strength I've become familiar with and I heard the words, "He's fine. Your son is fine." And in that instant, I began to breathe. I began to live my life once again. While I waited to see my son, I imagined his beautiful little face and I heard the words he's said so many times before, "Mommy, thank you for helping me." And all I could think to say was, "Thank you, Matthew, and thank you, God, for this journey."

TREVOR

Laura Hirsch

Six months pregnant with my second child, I was at the pediatrician's office with my three-year-old firstborn son, Trevor, for a routine visit. I was expecting the usual excellent progress report: Trevor is doing great, his development is ahead of the norm, and he is in perfect health. I had just completed his developmental chart, and as she read it, I detected some concern on Dr. Glickman's part and a change in her demeanor.

Although he did talk, I knew that Trevor was behind in speech development, and he had recently begun doing some odd behaviors such as lining up his toys, pulling people to get him what he needed, and making repetitive hand gestures as if he were playing with hand puppets. These things were nothing to be alarmed about, I reasoned. He'd begun walking and talking at nine months, and had reached all of his other developmental milestones early. I just thought that he was a late bloomer when it came to fluent communication, or that boys talk later than girls, or that the old saying "Early walker, late talker" was true in his case.

Trevor was my first child. Knowing little about child development, I trusted other mothers who told me not to worry about it, he'd be fine, so-and-so didn't talk until he was four, and he's fine.

"I am concerned about Trevor because his development has not progressed much in the past year, and his speech is severely delayed," Dr. Glickman hesitantly began. "What does that mean?" I asked as my heart began to race. My mom, who was our live-in nanny, was with us and was now hanging on the young doctor's every word. "It could just be developmental delay, and he will be just fine. My husband didn't talk until he was three, and he's fine," she said reassuringly. "But what's the worst-case scenario?" I demanded. My whole perception of the room shifted and I felt as if I had been transported to another dimension, no longer in the doctor's office but in a tunnel with me at one end and the doctor at the other. Everything in the room darkened and faded from sight. I felt faint.

The doctor continued, "Now before I say the word, I want to tell you that it is a spectrum disorder, with some cases very severe and detected at birth, while others are on the mild end of the spectrum and very high functioning." "What is it?" I pleaded. Before she even said the words, I clearly heard the word autism whispered in my ear, as if I had some sort of inner knowing. Next, I saw Dr. Glickman's mouth open, and the words came at me down the tunnel in slow motion: "Autistic spectrum disorder." There, she'd finally said it.

The room returned to normal, and I chalked it up to some weird pregnancy thing. The doctor continued to talk, but I barely heard a word she said. I looked over at my sweet, blond-haired, blue-eyed angel sitting on my mom's lap and knew that the doctor had to be wrong. She referred me to a developmental pediatrician

who specialized in this area and told me I could call her at home
if she could help out in any way. She was going to be the pediatrician of my unborn child as well and was very involved. She actually admitted to me later that telling me, a woman six months
pregnant, that her three year old may have autism, was the hardest
thing she ever had to do as a doctor.

As we left the pediatrician's office, I immediately started
going through the grief process. I was in deep shock. What had
just happened? Yesterday he was a perfect little boy, and today he
may or may not have autism? The only thing I really knew about
autism was from Dustin Hoffman's portrayal of an autistic adult
in the movie Rain Man, and there was no way Trevor was like that.

As soon as we got home, I called my younger sister, Kim, and
told her what had just happened at the doctor's office. We were
living in California, and she lived in Illinois, but she had seen
Trevor on at least a half dozen occasions and heard all about him
every week from me. She also said, "There's no way." We hung up
the phone and each secretly went on the Internet and searched for
everything we could find out about autism. When I called her back
to tell her what I'd found, she admitted that she had also looked
it up online. We compared notes, and neither of us believed, or
wanted to believe, that Trevor fit this diagnosis. This was the
beginning of denial. I felt a bit of relief after making this decision,
but something was still not right. Some of the things I read
sounded like Trevor. What if?

I called to make an appointment with the specialist that we
were referred to, only to find out that she had a six-month waiting
list. I couldn't wait that long to find out what was wrong with my
precious son. I called Dr. Glickman back, and she referred me to a
speech pathologist, Nancy, who worked from her home. I immediately called Nancy, and in my panic was hoping she would give

me a diagnosis over the phone based on my description of his behavior. She could sense my concern but said that she had to do an evaluation in person. We set it up for September 11, 2001. I will never forget that day for more than the obvious reason.

After watching the television in disbelief as the Twin Towers came crashing down, I called Nancy to see if Trevor's appointment was still on. Little did I know that the rest of my world was about to come crashing down around me as well. After Trevor's evaluation, Nancy still wouldn't give me her diagnosis. I had to wait for her to mail it to me. The waiting was absolute agony, and when it arrived, I almost shredded the envelope trying to get to the paper. It still didn't give me any concrete answers. I skipped right to the conclusion section of the report, which said that she felt that it was more than just delayed speech, possibly autistic spectrum disorder or pervasive developmental disorder (PDD). She recommended that I take Trevor to a public school in our area for special needs children because they did further evaluations for free, and had special programs for children over the age of three.

The grief process continued, and did I ever know about grief. I had lost my first husband six years earlier at the age of twenty-seven in a car accident, and was actually writing a book at the time about my experience. I was seeing a familiar parallel between the loss of a loved one and what I was now experiencing with the possibility of having a special needs child. I felt that God was playing some kind of a cruel joke on me. Now, I had to grieve over the loss of the child I thought I had, and come to accept the child that I actually did have. I didn't even know who that was.

In the anger phase of grief I looked for someone to blame. I was mad at myself for not recognizing the signs sooner. Was it something that I had done before or during my pregnancy that had caused this? Had I been too busy doing other things? Was I just such a horrible mother? I felt guilty because I hadn't realized what was going on, and because I got mad at him and frustrated when he couldn't tell me what he wanted. I thought, if this was genetic, maybe this was my husband's fault. Was someone in his family autistic? Was someone in mine? Maybe I was the one with bad genes. What about the baby I am carrying? Would he or she be affected as well? I couldn't stop questioning everything.

I was also mad at God. Hadn't I suffered enough over losing my first husband at such a young age? Now, I was expecting a new baby in a month, and I didn't even know what Trevor's future held. I started to bargain with God. I would not go back to work and would instead spend all of my time with Trevor if he would only make him better. "This isn't fair! I can't handle any more pain," I cried out to God.

I had a total regression and became depressed again watching the grieving, pregnant widows from the September 11 tragedies telling their stories. It brought back my feelings of widowhood with a vengeance, and fueled the fire of the grief I was now experiencing over my new tragedy with my beloved son's possible diagnosis. At times, I didn't know whom I was crying for — the people on television, my late husband, Trevor, or myself. I had to stop watching the news because I figured that the daily crying jags couldn't be good for my unborn child or for me. Before the baby was born, I had to take action to try to help Trevor. I feared that he was going to slip away from me if I didn't do something fast. Remaining in a state of denial would do him no good.

I made an appointment with the school and had Trevor evaluated there. Still, no formal diagnosis was given, although insinuations were made heavily toward either autistic spectrum disorder or pervasive developmental disorder, which is another way of saying mild autism. Why was everyone so afraid to be honest and tell me the truth? Was it because I was pregnant, or was it because they just couldn't say for certain this early on? Trevor was placed in one of the school's programs where he would get the speech therapy and socialization he needed.

After being in the school for a few months, I wanted to get Trevor some outside speech therapy in addition to what the school was providing. I took him for an evaluation with a speech therapist recommended by a mother I met at Trevor's school. After the thirty-minute evaluation, I casually asked the therapist for a diagnosis since no one else would give me any concrete answers. She nonchalantly replied, "I'd say he's somewhere in the autistic spectrum." Her words felt like a knife plunging into my heart. That same night, after being on the verge of tears all day, I went to a parents' support group meeting at Trevor's school, alone, since my husband was more in denial than I was and didn't feel the need to go to a support group. On the drive to the school, when I heard Celine Dion's song about her newborn son, "A New Day Has Come," I totally lost it, sobbing the whole way there and talking between sobs during most of the meeting as well. I felt that a new day had come for me as well. I was beginning a new journey I never planned on taking.

After Trevor attended only six months at the new school, my husband got a great job offer in Reno, Nevada, and we decided to make the move and start all over again. I was secretly hoping that all of these people in California had been wrong about Trevor, and that when we got to Nevada, I would be told that he was going to be just fine.

Trevor was placed in a preschool classroom for children with developmental delay, close to the house we were renting. I drove him there and picked him up every day. In Nevada, since the school district doesn't label children until they are six, again we dealt with developmental delay, hinting all the while at autistic spectrum disorder. This helped me in my denial. In between caring for Trevor and his now six-month-old brother, Damon, I started reading everything I could get my hands on about autism and related disorders. I was also working part-time as a makeup artist and trying to find a house to buy. However, helping Trevor was still my top priority. I had to become a detective to try to unravel this mystery.

I started reading about sensory integration dysfunction, particularly the book, *The Out-of-Sync Child* by Carol Stock Kranowitz. The children she described in this book sounded a lot like Trevor to me. Their senses were not functioning normally, and their over- or undersensitivity interfered with communication and socialization. I began to realize that many of Trevor's odd behaviors over the past two years had been caused by his hypersensitive sensory system, most notably, his oversensitivity to sound. I looked back, and things started to make more sense.

Q: Why did Trevor cry or fuss when we got in the car?

A: The speakers were right by his car seat, and the rock music I preferred probably didn't help any.

Q: Why was Trevor afraid of the ocean?

A: The sound of the waves must have been frightening to him.

Q: Why did Trevor object to my singing when I rocked him to sleep?

A: The volume or pitch of my voice bothered him.

Q: Why did Trevor fuss, and say, "No! No!" when we went shopping at certain stores in the mall?

A: The music was too loud and hurt his ears.

Q: Why did Trevor cry and melt down when his cousin, Nicholas, was in the car?

A: He had a loud voice and unpredictably screamed a lot.

Q: Why was Trevor terrified of the rides at Disneyland?

A: The music and noise of the rides bothered him, along with the movement.

Q: Why did Trevor hum so much?

A: Humming masked other sounds and made him feel in control. It was obvious that Trevor covered his ears so often because certain noises bothered him.

Q: Why did Trevor scream and run away holding his ears whenever his brother Damon even entered the room?

A: Damon is the loudest child on the planet, and Trevor was anticipating an outburst.

Q: Why did Trevor pretend to be deaf at times, not answering to his own name?

A: He was tuning us all out.

Q: Why did Trevor cover his ears and run and hide when we used the blender, vacuum cleaner, and lawn mower?

A: They were too loud for him to be near.

Q: Why did he tremble with fear and cry when we went through the car wash?

A: He probably felt as if the car were going to cave in from the noise.

Q: Why did Trevor protest when we went to get his haircut? He let me cut it at home with scissors.

A: The buzzing of the clippers around his ears
     frightened him or hurt his ears.

With my new understanding of some of Trevor's main issues,
I took him to a place in town to have him evaluated for sensory
integration dysfunction. Although our health insurance didn't
cover the sensory integration therapy they offered, at least I had
some more answers, but alas, also more questions. I had Trevor's
hearing tested twice through the school district, and even though
they could only do limited testing, they concluded both times that
his hearing was within normal limits. Could it be, I asked myself,
that he has too much hearing? Or does he just process sound
differently?

I wasn't as interested anymore in what caused Trevor's difficulties or how people wanted to label him. I was just interested in
trying to help him get through his challenges as well as possible.
There is no test for autism, PDD, or sensory integration dysfunction. They are all diagnosed by observation, and the results are
highly subjective. The diagnosis depends on the observer, the honesty of the parents' answers, and the child's mood that day. The
label doesn't matter as much as the treatment of the symptoms.
Who knew my son better than I did? No one. I knew that there
was a bright child inside of him just waiting to come out. Ever
since he was two years old, he had been able to recite the alphabet.
He knew all of the letters independently and could count to
twenty and backward from ten to one. He knew his colors and
shapes and had over 250 words in is vocabulary. However, he
couldn't carry on a conversation and had almost no interest in
other children. His main trouble seemed to be the challenge of
sorting out sensory input.

I learned a great deal about occupational therapy and sensory integration therapy from information I received from Erin, Trevor's occupational therapist at school, and at the facility where our health insurance covered minimal sessions of speech therapy and occupational therapy. I started doing a lot of activities at home with Trevor for sensory integration, and we worked on his speech all day long, mainly through play-based therapy. Even with school, speech therapy, occupational therapy, and all of the work I was doing at home with him, I still felt that there was a big piece of the puzzle that was still missing.

My husband and I went to a parent training class called *More Than Words*, the workshop part of the Hanen Program. It taught us techniques to get Trevor to communicate in alternative ways. We were using the PECS system for a while, a picture exchange system for facilitating language. Soon, he began saying the words and outgrew the need for the PECS cards. At the parent training class I met a group of mothers of autistic children who stayed in touch with each other after the class ended to share information and offer moral support. We have meetings, e-mail each other, and occasionally have guest speakers with relevant information for the group.

A woman named Khymberleigh Herwill-Levin spoke at one of our meetings. She was an auditory integration training (AIT) therapist, a treatment that was supposed to desensitize hearing. Unfortunately, I wasn't able to make it to the meeting, but I was very interested in finding out more about AIT. I had recently read an article in our local paper featuring Khymberleigh talking about her success with AIT, especially with children with autism and PDD. I received some e-mails from the other moms about the information from the meeting, and decided to give Khymberleigh a call to find out more about AIT. Something was telling me that this might be something that would help Trevor.

Khymberleigh lived about an hour away but was going to be coming to Reno in a few weeks to treat a few other children, and had another opening if we were interested. We talked for a while and she mailed me an information packet and referred me to some websites to look up with more information about AIT. She suggested I talk with a parent of a boy who had recently been treated. Everything was pointing to doing AIT and I could not find a reason not to try it. It was one of those now or never situations because Trevor was on summer break from school, the timing was perfect, and Khymberleigh was going to be in town. If we waited, we would have to drive an hour a day, twice a day, for ten days. In addition, the training started on Trevor's fifth birthday, another good sign. To top it off, my husband, Matt, had just won an award in a sales contest at work, the cash equivalent of the cost of AIT. I am a big believer in receiving signs from above, and I knew that all of these were signs telling me to do it.

After discussing it with Matt, I called Khymberleigh and told her that we had decided to proceed with AIT. I was so excited. My only concern was whether or not Trevor would keep the headphones on or not. At Khymberleigh's suggestion, I purchased a pair of headphones and a CD of *Sesame Street* songs that Trevor knew. Gradually, after a few days, he went from not letting me put them on his head at all to listening to the CD for ten minutes at a time. It wasn't thirty minutes, but it was a start.

Everything about AIT made perfect sense to me. I believe that as a parent you intuitively know what treatments are right for your child, and which ones aren't. There are so many different programs available, so many different methods, and each one is not right for every child. But something about this resonated with me. I wasn't looking to cure him immediately, but my hope was that it might help him cope better with the world around him, which seemed to be intolerable at times. How can a child possibly be calm and expect to learn when he is constantly being bombarded by competing noises and sensory overload? I didn't want to look back one day and regret not doing this for my child when the opportunity was available, and to have to say, "What if I had done it?" The things that people regret most in life are the things that they didn't do.

A few days before Trevor's AIT began, I bought a book I had seen mentioned quite a bit in my AIT Internet research, *Sound of a Miracle* by Annabel Stehli. It was about her experience of raising her autistic daughter, Georgiana, who received AIT in France at age eleven, had a miraculous recovery from autism, and now as an adult had a college degree with honors, spoke six languages, and was married and a mother. I read the book in one day; I couldn't put it down. I was even reading parts of it out loud to my mom because so much of Georgie's hearing sensitivity described in the book sounded just like Trevor. For the first time in two years I could see a light at the end of the tunnel. I was so impressed with the story, so inspired, that I was filled with confidence that AIT might just be the missing piece of the puzzle I had been searching for.

The day before Trevor's AIT began, I went to our church and filled out a prayer request card for him. Our church has a Ministry of Prayer, and I enlisted them to pray for him, and that AIT would help desensitize his hearing. I received a letter from them a few days later confirming that the prayers had begun on the day the request was made and would continue for the next thirty days. I figured that we needed all the prayers we could get, so I also enlisted some friends and family members to pray for Trevor as well. I believe in the power of prayer, and with all of us praying for him, I was sure that AIT was going to bring results.

It was finally the big day. I was filled with excitement, hope, and worry all at once. My stomach had butterflies. I was still concerned about Trevor wearing the headphones and hoped that he wouldn't protest to the point that we would have to give up and try this again at a later date. The sessions were held on the second floor of an office building. I hoped that the walls were soundproofed in case Trevor became upset. We met Khymberleigh, and talked for a few minutes. I asked Khymberleigh what we needed to do to make him accept the headphones. She assured me that by the third day he would be sitting in the chair by himself and would leave them on. However, I might have to hold him down until he realized that they wouldn't hurt him, that it was just music. I hoped that she was right.

I had to physically restrain him while Khymberleigh placed the headphones on his wiggling head. Although he didn't struggle while sitting on my lap, he basically screamed for the whole thirty minutes. When people in the next room pounded on the wall, Khymberleigh went over to explain what all the noise was. They thought that there was a cat in the room screaming. I had to laugh at that one.

I felt horrible just letting Trevor scream, but I kept telling myself that this was for his own good and that it was going to get better next time. On the drive over for the second session, I kept praying for a sign that this was the right thing to do after the first stressful session. The second session went much better. He did the cat scream for the first ten minutes, and then he did great for the last twenty minutes. He played with toys, sat on my lap, and even stood up at the end and walked around. I was so relieved. This might not be so bad after all.

I got the sign I'd been praying for when we got home from the second session. Matt was mowing the front lawn as we were pulling into the garage, and I expected Trevor to hold his ears and run in the house when he got out of the minivan. I said, "Let's go in the house Trevor." He said, "No," and without covering his ears, he proceeded to go over to the lawnmower to help Matt finish the lawn. Matt and I looked at each other with our mouths hanging wide open. I was almost in tears. I yelled in the house for my mom to see what Trevor was doing. I stood on the porch and watched my son in awe as he pushed the lawnmower for the first time. I said a silent prayer of thanks, sure that AIT was the right thing to do.

I didn't expect to see results this quickly, as we had only completed two out of the twenty sessions. Also, I knew that many children didn't show improvement for months afterward, if at all. We were off to a good start, I thought. During the second day of AIT, Trevor did an awesome job of leaving his headphones on during both sessions, and at each session that followed as well. He sat in the chair by himself and played quietly with Play-doh the whole time. He was such a champ. I was so proud of him. He slept for twelve hours straight that night. He usually woke up a couple of times during the night. Wouldn't this be a bonus? He'd finally get some sleep, and so would I.

After the third day of AIT, I began to notice some other small changes. We were playing his computer game, and he was saying some words more clearly than he had in the past. He used to leave off the front "s" in the words "sneakers" and "skis." They sounded like "neakers" and "keys." Now he was saying them both correctly. I praised him, and when the game ended, he asked to go outside and jump. We got him a twelve-foot trampoline for his birthday, and he loved it. So did I, being a former gymnast. We had lots of fun on it. We went outside, and I put him up on the trampoline and stood next to it as a spotter. He kept saying, "Git-ball." I thought that he was labeling the small basketball that was next to me on the ground. I said a few times, "Yes, that is a basketball." After a few more tries, he walked right up to me, looked me in the eye, and said, "Get ball," and then looked at the ball. I understood. "Oh, you want me to get the ball?" He had never initiated play with the ball. I was shocked. For the next thirty minutes, we played a game of catch with him on the trampoline and me on the ground.

Later, he stood on the trampoline talking to himself and I was able to make out some of his jargon. He was reciting a line from his computer game. There is a gargoyle by the castle in the game who says, "I can do anything," and then flaps its wings, falls backward off the post, and screams, "Aagh," flies back up, and says, "Almost anything." I repeated what Trevor said after he said, "I can do anything." He looked at me as if to say, "You understood me?" He yelled "Aagh!" and did a backdrop onto the trampoline, stood up, and looked at me to finish. I said, "Almost anything." He laughed hysterically. This turn-taking game went on for about fifteen minutes. He started by saying, "I can do . . ." and I would say, "Anything." He would fall back screaming, "Aagh!" and I would finish the game by saying, "Almost anything." It was incredible. I had waited five years to have my son as a playmate, and now he was actually initiating play with me, not the other way around.

When we got inside, my brother Joey called to see how the AIT sessions were going. While I was telling him about all of the incredible things that had already happened, Trevor was trying to get me to chase him by saying, "Go!" I told Joey that I had better go play with Trevor since he was the one who was initiating it. As usual, I tried to get Trevor to say "good-bye." Usually he says no and pushes the phone away or just ignores me. This time, he clearly said, "Good-bye Joey, good-bye Joey." "Did you hear him?" I asked Joey. "Oh, my God, I can't believe it," he replied. I hung up the phone and chased and tickled Trevor until we were too tired to continue.

After each of the remaining days that followed, he did things at home after his two sessions of AIT that he had not done before. One day after AIT, I was sitting on the couch reading a book and Trevor was sitting on the floor next to me on a pile of pillows leaning on the arm of the couch and watching a videotape. Khymberleigh let me borrow her copy of *Overcoming Autism*, by Georgiana Thomas, Annabel Stehli's daughter. I was trying to get some insight into what might be going on inside of Trevor's head, from someone who had been there before, and was also old enough when she had AIT to be able to tell the differences before and after the training. As I was reading, I noticed that Trevor was staring at me, something he doesn't usually do. I looked over at him and he said, "Hi." I said, "Hi," back to him. He was totally checking me out, looking at my eyes, nose, and mouth, and touching my hair. He put my hand on his face and lay on my lap, still looking at me intensely. It was as if a fog had lifted from around him and he was seeing me clearly for the first time. It was a very touching moment.

Another wonderful change in Trevor during the week of AIT was that he was actually including his little brother in his play. He let Damon in his room and let him jump on his bed with him. Damon was twenty-one months old and perfectly fine, by the way, and he wanted to be everywhere that his big brother was, but Trevor usually slammed his door in Damon's face and said, "No, Damon." Trevor not only let Damon in, he tackled Damon on his bed and grabbed his hand, moving it to touch his own face.

Damon thought this was funny, and the two of them went back and forth taking turns giggling. Trevor also wanted Damon to participate in the "Go!" game that we play. Usually Damon would just join in on his own, but now Trevor invited him into his world by pulling on Damon's arm and saying, "Go!" It was wonderful to see them interacting.

A few days later, Trevor was playing on my bed with Damon, giggling and looking at him, taking turns getting thrown on the bed. Usually Trevor didn't want to share his playtime with him, but now Damon was fun, not the loud boy that hurt Trevor's ears. That same day after Damon woke up from his nap, Trevor walked into his room with me, saying, "Hi Damon." I was so happy to hear that. When we went into the living room, Trevor picked up some inflated bags he liked to play with and threw them in the air. He grabbed Damon's arm to pull him close to him, threw the bags, and pulled Damon down to the floor with him as the bags floated down on top of them. They giggled and looked at each other as if they were sharing an inside joke. They did it a few more times together before Damon was bored. It was so wonderful to see Trevor having fun with Damon.

I also saw many changes in his speech. He was repeating a lot more words and expressions upon request. At the first AIT session, Khymberleigh said that the only things she understood him saying were "No," and "Wash hands." By the end of the ten days, his speech was much clearer, and after Khymberleigh prompted him, he said, "Hi," "Good-bye Kimmy," "Thank you," and "See you later." He even gave her a hug and a kiss each day.

He said a lot of new words during the ten days of treatment and repeated a lot of words I was saying, over and over again to try to say them more clearly. He was also using longer sentences. One day, I asked him if he wanted a pickle. "No," he said. I asked again for clarity, "You don't want a pickle?" "Don't want a pickle," he answered. Five syllables. He also started using the word "want" in front of things that he wanted. He usually just said "drink" when he wanted a drink. Now he was walking up to me and saying, "Want drink," without prompting.

He also began initiating a lot more speech instead of just echolalia or labeling. He came into my bathroom one day carrying two CDs in his hands that he'd taken from the CD tower in my bedroom. After standing there for a few minutes, he said, "Turn off." I had the radio on, and always turned it off just before I left the room. I said, "Turn off the music?" "Turn off music," he repeated, pulling me over to the CD tower. "Put away," he said. "Oh, you want me to put these away for you?" This type of verbal exchange never happened before. In the past, he would just stand there and whine.

He interacted more with people who are not family members. I took him to speech therapy twice and occupational therapy once after his AIT, and each time he said, "Hi," and "Good-bye," calling people by name, giving them big hugs, and letting them kiss him on the cheek. They were stunned. A woman named Elf, who handles the insurance, has always shown a particular interest in Trevor. When Trevor said, "Good-bye, Elf," and gave her a giant hug, I thought she was going to cry. She knew he had just had AIT and she saw the progress he has made in such a short time.

We stopped to buy dog food on the way home a few days after his AIT ended. Trevor had only been in this store once before, a few months earlier. As soon as we walked in the door, he said, "Sucker," and started to look behind the counter. I usually carry suckers with me, and I said, "I don't have any suckers, honey." He went around to the other side of the counter and repeated, "Sucker." The owner of the store said, "Oh, I probably gave him a sucker last time he was here," and reached under the counter for a tin canister. She pulled out three suckers including a red one, the only color he likes. She asked him what color he wanted. Instinctively, I answered for him, "Red." "No, orange," Trevor said, and proceeded to take the orange sucker from her hand. He dutifully said, "thank you," when I asked him to. Usually he said nothing. I was stunned. "I can't believe he remembered that," I said to the owner, "or that he picked orange." "Oh, yeah, kids always remember the suckers," she said. He began to follow dog footprints painted on the floor. He looked at me and said, "footprints." The owner also pointed out the nose prints on the window. He looked and said, "nose prints." After she rang up my purchase, she said good-bye to Trevor, and he took the sucker out of his mouth to say good-bye. We got into the car where my mom and Damon were waiting for us and I said to my mom, "You are not going to believe what Trevor just did."

Writing this a month after Trevor completed his AIT therapy, that is how a lot of my conversations are beginning these days: "You're not going to believe what Trevor just did, or said." The list of firsts is getting longer and longer. About two weeks after AIT ended, I was putting Trevor to bed and as usual, I brought him to both Matt and my mom to say good-night. They always say, "I love you, Trevor," in addition to giving him a good night kiss, which Trevor always accepts on the cheek instead of the lips. This particular night, after receiving his kiss on the cheek, Trevor said, "I love you, Daddy," to Matt, and "I love you, Grandma," for the first time to my mom. She was so touched she was almost crying. She had been waiting for five years to hear him say that.

I took Trevor in to bed (I usually lie down with him until he falls asleep), and as we were lying there, Trevor initiated giving me a kiss, on the lips! He leaned in toward me and said, "Kiss,"

and kissed me twice on the cheek. "Kiss," he said again, and proceeded to kiss me on the lips. I could probably count on one hand
how many times he had kissed me on the lips in the past, and he
actually initiated it this time. I couldn't believe it. He made us all
happy that night.

I started keeping a journal of his post-AIT progress to send
to mothers who were eagerly awaiting our results. I was not expecting so much so soon, but I'm not complaining. Aside from the
things I have already mentioned, the following is a list of other
changes and improvements that we have seen either during the ten
days of AIT or in the month that followed:

- He is calmer and less fussy. He still has his moments, but
  there is improvement. He wakes up happy in the morning
  too, which is new.
- He is cuddlier, and seeks more affection and attention.
  He is giving full frontal contact body hugs, not the usual
  turn to the side variety, and is even snuggling his face in my
  neck and cuddling with me cheek to cheek. This has been
  wonderful.
- He is much more involved and interested in what is going
  on around him and wants to interact with everyone in
  the family, and to be included in everything, instead of
  wanting to be left alone all the time.
- He is constantly requesting games or activities that involve
  other people. His favorite thing used to be watching video-
  tapes; he would ask for specific ones and watched certain
  parts over and over. He has not asked to watch one tape
  since we started AIT. Although he will watch a tape for a
  while if Damon has one on, Trevor prefers to be chased
  and tickled or thrown on the bed. He wants to go outside

and jump on the trampoline, or to go to the pool. Rather than being passive and waiting for us to dictate which activities were going to take place, he's showing preferences and verbally initiating activities he wants to do.

- He is showing everyone more eye contact, has a bigger appetite, and is requesting a wider variety of foods. He requested and ate ten Chicken McNuggets three days in a row during AIT. The most he had eaten before that was three or four.

- He is sleeping better and longer, ten to twelve hours a night. He doesn't seem as bothered by the sounds that used to make him cover his ears, like the garage door opener and the hair dryer. He even let me blow-dry his hair one day. He also put his ear on the speaker of his piano keyboard on the loudest setting. He used to have to cover one ear with one hand and the other ear with his shoulder while he played with that hand because it was too loud for him, even with the volume turned down.

- He is following verbal directions better. If I ask him to bring me something, he does. I tested him, saying, "Go ask grandma to give you a drink." He walked downstairs and asked her for a drink.

- He is doing less self-stimulatory behavior, specifically nail biting, and is showing less tactile defensiveness. During a session of occupational therapy he let Erin brush his hair (a form of sensory therapy) without resisting, and he touched and played with therapy putty and waxy sticks for the first time. He had refused to touch them in the past.

- He now says good-bye to people by name on the telephone. One funny story here: Khymberleigh called to see how Trevor was doing after his AIT, and he was in the background saying, "Go!" trying to get me to chase him. I told him that I would chase him when I was off the phone. After a few more futile attempts with "Go!" he came over to me and said, "Good-bye, Uncle Joey," assuming that was who I was talking to, since I usually ask Trevor to say good-bye to him. Khymberleigh and I shared a good laugh over his cleverness.

- He is answering more yes or no questions and making a selection when given a choice. He is more interested in playing with toys and books and plays with toys appropriately, a first. He even takes toys away from Damon that he wants to play with, not something a mother normally rejoices in, but in this case, I do.

- He will say a word, wait for me to repeat it, and say another word for me to repeat. The other day he named all of the characters from *Jay Jay the Jet Plane* and waited for me to say them after he did.

- He is much more aware of what is going on around him. He hates it and cries whenever I leave the room and wants to be wherever I am. Usually, I could leave the room without his noticing. Now he runs over and follows me.

- He is becoming interested in other children. At the open gym gymnastics class, he actually noticed the other kids around him and tried to play with them. He was laughing and jumping on the trampoline with one little girl and had a verbal exchange with another child. Previously he ignored everyone.

- He is asking people other than me to play with him and care for him. A few weeks after AIT, Trevor was in the master bedroom with Matt and me and said, "Throw me." I figured he wanted me to do it but he pushed me aside, saying, "Daddy throw me." Matt was so happy, as he often feels rejected by Trevor's preference for me all of the time. They played together for a while, and Trevor let Matt give him his bath. When he got out of the tub, Trevor kissed Matt on the lips. Matt was almost in tears. He is finally feeling as if he has a relationship with his son.

• He began playing his computer game by himself. About a month after AIT, Trevor and I were playing his computer game at his request. Usually, I operate the mouse, and he tells me where he would like to go on the screen. I had to excuse myself and told him I would be right back. To my amazement, I heard him continuing the game on his own. Trevor suddenly put it all together and figured out how to move the mouse, navigate around the screen, and click and drag the mouse to play the game by himself. When I returned, he finished playing the game alone, matching items, sorting like items, listening and following directions. Now he always wants to do it by himself. I am still in shock over this huge accomplishment.

To summarize, I cannot attribute all of these changes within a short thirty-day time period to anything other than AIT. I could understand, if I hadn't seen changes immediately, that it would be hard to say for sure whether the changes were because of simple maturation, other therapies, or a combination of things. But he was out of school during this time and had minimal outside therapies, so my conclusion is that all of these consecutive changes could only be the result of AIT. He had not shown this much progress in six months of therapy or a year of school. Suddenly, things are starting to click for Trevor. It is as if he is finally cracking the code of communication that so far has been difficult for him.

As far as the grief process goes, I would have to admit that it has taken two years, but I have finally accepted the fact that my child has special needs although I still have a hard time attaching a label to him. However, I don't look at it as a misfortune the way a lot of people would. I look at it as a gift. I take comfort in the fact that God sent Trevor here this way with a purpose, and that I was chosen to be his mom. I couldn't imagine him any other way. I feel that I have far more to learn from him than he does from me, including patience, tolerance, and unconditional love. Trevor's triumphs are so much sweeter than they would be for a child to whom things come naturally. I just swell with pride each time he does or says something new. And since AIT, I feel as if I am about to burst!

Trevor will be starting in a new school this fall, with teachers highly trained in autism and related disorders. He will also be receiving speech therapy and occupational therapy, and will have a lot of one-on-one attention in class, as there are only six students in the class. I believe that after having AIT, all the other therapies are going to come together, and I can see a bright future for my son. For lack of a better word, I would have to say that for Trevor, AIT has been nothing short of a miracle.

BRIAN

Colleen Whelan

When Brian was born weighing a whopping ten pounds, seven ounces, my husband, Mark, and I were ready to call Lou Holz and ink an early deal with "The Fighting Irish" of Notre Dame. Brian's sister, Meghan, was born just twenty-one months before him. We felt extremely blessed to have two beautiful, healthy children.

Brian was, for the most part, a good baby, quiet and independent, like his dad. He would play on his own for hours and demanded little attention. He did not need to be held to fall asleep as his sister had. He could just be put down in his crib with the lights out and the door shut. Sometimes when I'd hear him laugh and squeal with delight, I thought he must be talking to the angels.

Brian did, however, exhibit a great deal of anxiety around anyone other than Mark or me. Not even family members or friends were able to interact with him in any way. Even when his sister made attempts to play with him, he would push her away without even looking at her. At the time, we thought that he was simply attached to me and would grow out of it. He did not like to be held and read to as his sister had and he was not speaking as early as she had either. Everyone told us that we should not compare the two children because it was not uncommon for boys, especially when they were the second children, to develop language later.

At his eighteen-month check-up, Brian's pediatrician recommended that we have him screened by Connecticut's early intervention agency, Birth to Three, if he didn't have speech by his second birthday. The doctor was unable to conduct a thorough exam or ask many questions because Brian screamed, as he usually did, throughout the appointment.

That same week, I happened to see a friend of mine who is a speech and language pathologist. She advised me that, as eighteen to twenty-four months is an important time for language development, if Brian needed therapy, we should not put it off. She asked me questions about how Brian communicated, if he could follow simple commands such as: "Let's go" or "Wave bye-bye." He could not. She asked how he told me that he wanted something. I realized that he did not make any attempt to communicate, not even nonverbally. Rather, he would pull me to a desired object, using me as a tool to get what he wanted. Without realizing it, I was anticipating his needs and not requiring him to point or try to speak to me. We discussed how Brian played alone most of the time and had no interest in other children. After I told her that he loved cars and trucks, she asked if he made car sounds or pretended that they were being driven or crashing. Again, the answer was no. He would simply line them up and look at them.

Mark and I decided not to wait. We took Brian to an audiologist, who ruled out deafness and had him evaluated by Birth to Three. The results were devastating. Brian was severely delayed in every area of development. Although he was almost twenty months old, his language skills were at the level of a three month old and his social skills were at the level of a five month old. We knew that there was more here to worry about than a simple speech delay.

When my father asked me if Brian could be autistic, I dismissed it immediately because he did not act like the autistic man portrayed by Dustin Hoffman in Rain Man. My sister-in-law, who had worked with autistic children at Douglas College, told me that autistic children as young as Brian often look completely normal. She had noticed things about Brian that concerned her. On a recent visit to their home, Brian had spent most of the time running back and forth in the same path while holding one arm in the air and repeating the only sound he ever made, "Da da da da." Preferring to be alone, he had showed no interest in his cousins, and he had failed to react when she purposefully tried to startle him. He had become extremely distressed when anyone went near him. He would focus on something intently and throw a terrible tantrum if you tried to take the object of his attention away. She noted that Brian also had strong attachments to strange things, like bars of soap or powder bottles, and she told us that these behaviors were typical of a child with autism. She recommended that Brian be seen by a neurologist. Had I known anything about autism, these now glaring signs might have meant something. But they didn't. We weren't intentionally dismissing anything but we hadn't been looking for anything either.

On April 17, 1998, we had an appointment with a neurologist in Danbury, Connecticut, to rule out autism or any other neurological cause for Brian's delays. Brian and I were in one car while Mark drove in his. Mark would go straight to work once our worries were laid to rest. Ah, those last minutes of denial and acting as if we could make it not true by acting as if it weren't. We were within minutes of the doctor's office when I admitted to myself what I had already known, that in my heart I knew that our lives were about to change. It was a sinking feeling that I will never forget.

Brian screamed relentlessly as he tried to escape from the neurologist and he spent as much time as possible running back and forth in the hallway. We showed the doctor the evaluations completed by Birth to Three. We discussed, in detail, all of our concerns. Based on the previous evaluations and on his own observations, the neurologist explained that Brian met more than the minimum criteria for a diagnosis of autism. He had no doubt that it was an appropriate diagnosis.

Through our tears, we barely listened to the doctor as he described the special schools Brian would need. He said that most autistics never gain meaningful communication and that even if Brian did learn to speak, "He'll never be a politician." We were told that ritalin and prozac were available and that Brian would need blood work to determine if he had Fragile X, which is genetically based mental retardation. I was also assured that I had not caused his autism. I was surprised that the doctor mentioned this because the thought that I could have inflicted this on my child had never entered my mind. I soon learned that the prevailing wisdom, until the 1960s when Bernard Rimland wrote a book dismissing the notion, was that autism was caused by cold, "refrigerator" mothers.

After learning that there was no known cause or cure for Brian's autism, we were left with no plan of action to treat him. Our sadness was overwhelming. How our hearts broke for our little boy and for the future we were told he would never have.

The next day was a Saturday and my husband pulled everything he could find on autism off the Internet. So much of what we read was contradictory. Even the so-called experts did not agree on which, if any, treatments or therapies would help. The one thing we did become convinced of was that early intervention was crucial. The fact that Brian was diagnosed at only twenty-one months was in our favor. His brain was not yet fully developed and therefore had "plasticity." Intense therapy, we hoped, could help his brain make the appropriate connections and possibly reverse the course of his autism!

Our sense of grief was pushed aside by a sense of urgency. On Monday morning we called the Autism Research Institute in San Diego and requested information. They sent articles and studies describing various interventions that had helped relieve autistic symptoms in many cases. Among the therapies described were high doses of vitamin B6, magnesium, N,N-dimethlglycine (DMG), and a diet free of gluten and casein. They included research showing the effectiveness of intensive early intervention. Most notable was a method of intensive behavioral therapy called Applied Behavior Analysis (ABA), which involved breaking down skills into simple commands utilizing reinforcement and data collection. We ordered books on ABA along with samples of the nutritional supplements.

On Thursday we headed to New Jersey, where my family lived. We were taking Brian to a priest my parents knew from daily Mass. He was going to say a prayer of healing for Brian at 3:00 in the afternoon, which we coordinated with a request to friends and family to pray at the exact same time. We would "storm heaven" as we asked for God's help. The priest said, when we got there, that he had been praying for Brian and that God had a message for us. He said, "You know how much you love your son . . . God wants you to know that He loves him even more." These were the first words that had brought me any comfort, and I have thought of them and trusted in them many times in the last five years. He went on to say that God would heal Brian in His own time and way and that God wanted to be glorified through us. Although we weren't going to get the instant and complete resolution we wanted, we would get our miracle.

In the week before we met with the priest, I had read *Let Me Hear Your Voice* by Catherine Maurice, describing a little girl's recovery from autism with ABA. Although we were sure we wanted to try ABA, knowing what we wanted to do and actually doing it were two completely different things. While the state of Connecticut would fund up to thirty hours a week of home therapy under Brian's diagnosis, people trained to provide ABA were not available. We would have to find people and train them to work with Brian ourselves. Had we still been living in New Jersey, where I had family, friends, and connections, it would have been easier. As it was, I was feeling isolated and disconnected in the rural section of Connecticut where we had moved the previous year. I compared it at the time to finding out that your child needs brain surgery. The skilled surgeon is unavailable so you have to determine the best method, take the knife, and do it yourself. How terrifying this was!

Six weeks after Brian's diagnosis, feeling overwhelmed and depressed, I said an extremely desperate prayer begging God to send me someone who could show me the way to help Brian. After using a prayer book a friend had just sent me, I put it down on a business card for the Georgiana Institute for Auditory Integration Training (AIT). I had been so focused on setting up Brian's ABA program that I had already moved this card several times among my quickly growing resources. AIT was something that I intended to look into down the road but not then. Something made me pick up the phone and call.

I left a message that was returned almost immediately by Annabel Stehli. Little did I know how much that call would change our lives. Annabel is the founder of the Institute, the author of *Sound of A Miracle*, and the editor of *Dancing in the Rain*. She lived only minutes away and offered to bring me her information in person. An hour later, the answer to my desperate prayer was sitting in my backyard sharing a lifetime of knowledge and experience with me.

Annabel felt that Brian's coloring indicated nutritional deficiencies. She also explained that his "odd" behaviors actually had meaning and most likely stemmed from sensory integration issues. She agreed that Brian needed intense, one-on-one behavioral therapy and she recommended a modified approach, combining theories from the Option Institute and ABA as developed by Ivar Lovaas. She referred to it as "Lovaas with Love." Annabel also explained that painful hearing is often at the root of an autistic person's seeming inability to learn or communicate. She recommended AIT as a means of retraining Brian's hearing through the use of filtered and modulated music. I learned that the nerves of the inner ear are flexible and that the degree of abnormal hearing can be lessened with sessions that last for half an hour, twice a day, for ten days. Because of the profound impact that AIT had had on Annabel's daughter, Georgie, I knew that this would be something we would try for Brian. Georgie's story, along with the new insight and understanding I gained about my son and his autism that day, made me feel empowered to help him.

I was reminded of *The Mountain*, an inspirational story by Jim Stovall that tells of two warring tribes in the Andes, one that lived in the lowlands and the other high in the mountains. The mountain people invaded the lowlanders one day, and as part of their plundering, they kidnapped a baby and took the infant with them back up into the mountains. The lowlanders didn't know how to climb the mountain. They didn't know any of the trails that the mountain people used, and they didn't know where to find the mountain people or how to track them in the steep terrain. Even so, they sent out their best party of fighting men to climb the mountain and bring the baby home.

The men tried first one method of climbing and then another. They tried one trail and then another. After several days of effort, they had climbed only a few hundred feet. Feeling hopeless and helpless, the lowlander men decided that the cause was lost and prepared to return to their village. As they were packing their gear for the descent, they saw the baby's mother walking toward them. They realized that she was coming down the mountain that they hadn't figured out how to climb. To their amazement they saw the baby strapped to her back. How could that be?

One man greeted her and said, "We couldn't climb this mountain. How did you do this when we, the strongest and most able men in the village, couldn't do it?"

She shrugged her shoulders. "It wasn't your baby," she said.

—⊷⊷—

Annabel gave me a list of AIT practitioners and noted that Sally Brockett of Idea, Inc., in West Haven was the most experienced in Connecticut. I called Sally right away and she came to our home the next week. We discussed ABA, AIT, behavioral optometry, nutrition, and cranio-sacral therapy. While discussing Brian's medical and developmental history, we told Sally that Brian's fontanels had closed when he was just four months old. X-rays were taken and evaluated by a neurologist, who advised us not to be concerned. He told us that as long as growth remained consistent, Brian would be fine. Sally examined Brian's head and pointed out distortions in his skull. She explained that proportion, and not just circumference, was important for brain growth and function.

Sally explained the *Hierarchy of Development*, indicating that underlying functions such as nutrient deficiencies, immune system malfunction, chemical sensitivities, inflammation, and allergies, as well as basic sensory channels, innate reflexes, gross motor coordination, and fine motor coordination must be corrected before you can fully develop cognitive and perceptual abilities. Sally agreed with Annabel that Brian's coloring was indicative of nutritional deficiencies.

Because Sally did not conduct AIT for children under three, we would focus on other issues over the coming year. She felt that this would actually help Brian be more receptive when he did receive AIT. She referred us to Dr. Richard Caskey, a chiropractic kinesiologist and certified licensed nutritionist. My husband was skeptical but his doubts were quickly erased. Dr. Caskey's knowledge of the effects of structure and nutrition on the body was impressive. To this day he continues to be our most trusted and respected resource for our entire family's nutritional health needs.

He confirmed the distortions to Brian's skull and explained that the pressure to Brian's right temporal lobe could be affecting Brian's language development. He also regarded information — dismissed by other doctors — as clues to the workings of Brian's body. It had never made sense to me that Brian could possibly be healthy despite the fact that I had suffered from severe nausea and dehydration through the first six months of my pregnancy. Although I had been unable to keep any food or even prenatal vitamins down, my obstetrician assured me that Brian would not be affected. Dr. Caskey felt otherwise. His high birthweight didn't guarantee that Brian had gotten what he needed from me. In fact, he probably had not. This, along with the fact that Brian had a very limited diet of mostly processed carbohydrates, indicated that Brian most likely suffered from nutritional deficiencies. As he had never tolerated milk-based formula and had been switched to soy as an infant, he most likely had a milk allergy.

Dr. Caskey conducted hair and urine analysis as well as a complete physical evaluation. He took a comprehensive history of Brian's health including vaccination and antibiotic use. The tests indicated low nutrient levels and high levels of metals, most notably aluminum. Dr. Caskey felt that these imbalances could be treated with nutritional therapy.

When we addressed Brian's high level of anxiety toward people, Dr. Caskey explained that Brian's adrenal system was not functioning properly. His body was stuck in "Fight-or-Flight" mode all the time. He started Brian on adrenal support, whole food medical supplements, and digestive enzymes. Brian responded almost immediately. Within two days, Brian understood and followed his first command. After months of trying to get him to wave bye-bye, he actually did it. With only my verbal command, he waved and he said "aye-aye," his first sounds other than "da, da, da." We were ecstatic! His eyes gradually became clearer and his coloring improved. It was as if the tank had been empty and was now filled up and ready to go.

The timing was perfect, as we had finally found the right person to head his home ABA program. Audra was an early intervention specialist with Connecticut's Birth to Three. She had an immediate and rare connection with Brian and had years of experience working with children with autism. Although I once questioned why we ended up away from family and friends at this time in our lives, in looking back, I know we were exactly where we needed to be. Audra was the first person Brian felt safe with other than his father and me. Even though he would protest when it was time to work, he would reach for Audra the minute she walked in the house. We had agreed on a program based on discreet trials with sessions seven mornings a week. We used the programs from Catherine Maurice's book, *Behavioral Intervention for Young Children with Autism*. Brian also responded well to Bonnie, his weekend therapist, experienced with autistic children like Audra but with a more developmental approach. Although she followed his behavioral program, she always noted the typical behaviors Brian had as a little boy.

Whenever possible, Brian had afternoon ABA sessions or speech therapy after his nap. He received deep pressure and brushing at the beginning of each session. When he was upset, joint compression helped to calm him. Whatever programs his therapists worked on, we were responsible for working into the rest of the day. This incidental learning and reinforcement are key, and his sister, Meghan, was an integral part of them. She imitated the language Audra used and reinforced any desired behavior or learning with praise and excitement. I'd be in another room and hear, "Good looking" or "Good pointing." She'd help with programs like turn-taking even though, in the beginning, it meant she had a three-second turn while Brian's was much longer. I always tell Meghan that Brian would not be where he is without her. I also took Brian to a "Mommy and me" gymnastics class.

One of the college students who helped Brian that summer noticed that he would watch television with his head tilted sideways. Her mom was a vision therapist and she told me that, as usual, this odd behavior had a purpose for Brian. He was actually turning off the lower eye when he tilted his head in order to reduce the amount of visual information he was taking in but could not process. To prove her point, when she had me cover the top eye, his head immediately straightened up, as he needed that other eye to see.

Brian also avoided direct eye contact. By using his peripheral vision he reduced the amount of visual stimulation he received. Looking back, I can recall an instance before we had suspected anything was wrong. Brian was on the changing table and I was trying to get him to look at me. I kept moving myself to be in his direct field of vision but he kept looking away. It must have been too much for him to process, and it was possibly even painful for him to look directly at me.

He had depth perception problems as well. He would get down and try to crawl off the carpet to the hardwood floor. Even though they were basically the same height, it was as if he were climbing down a step. No wonder he was so afraid of everyone. Imagine how scary and distorted people's faces must have looked to him!

We took him to a behavioral optometrist because we had read that prism glasses had helped children with visual processing issues. He did not feel that Brian needed the glasses or vision therapy. He suggested that the nutritional supplements Brian had recently begun taking would help. He was right. His visual processing problems corrected themselves.

Brian's extreme fear of others began to diminish and the adrenal support seemed to help him be able to calm himself when he did become distressed. He spent less and less time running back and forth and allowed others to hold and change him. He also began to accept and even seek out a broader diet that included protein like meat and eggs. The chiropractic and cranio-sacral therapy were producing changes in the shape of his skull.

Six months after his diagnosis, Brian went to Sidney Baker,

M.D., for his first infusion of secretin. Dr. Baker, a leading clini-
cian in the held of autism, is the author of *Detoxification and Healing*,
The Circadian Prescription, and the coauthor of *The DAN! Protocol*.
Secretin is a naturally occurring enzyme that is deficient in many
children with autism. A mom, Victoria Beck, had discovered
secretin's benefit after her autistic son received it as a routine part
of an endoscopy. After much effort to obtain more secretin to
confirm its dramatic affects on her son's speech and behavior, she
shared her experience with the new treatment at a DAN!
Conference I had attended that same month. (DAN! stands for
"Defeat Autism Now!" and the movement and the protocol support research and provide biomedical assessment options for children with autism.)

Dr. Baker recommended that we remove all gluten and dairy
from Brian's diet immediately. He felt that it was more important
to get these foods out of Brian's body than to wait and see which
results, if any, came from the secretin infusions. We had already
purchased Lisa Lewis's book, *Special Diets for Special Kids*, and began
the dietary changes right away. Lisa's book gives a clear and easy-
to-understand explanation of how the undigested proteins from
gluten and casein, called peptides, cause or contribute to a leaky
gut, crossing the blood-brain barrier to have an opiate effect on
the brain. It is also an excellent guide to actually feeding your child
on this diet. About three weeks after his first secretin infusion and
beginning a gluten/casein-free diet, Brian had a definite increase in
receptive language and was vocalizing more.

Dr. Baker also suggested that Brian might benefit from an
antifungal treatment. Dr. Caskey agreed and ordered a stool test
that confirmed an overgrowth of intestinal yeast called candida
most likely resulting from antibiotics killing off the good bacteria
as well as the bad. The absence of good bacteria is as alarming as

the overgrowth of yeast for several reasons as the good bacteria is necessary for proper absorption of nutrients and is responsible for keeping bad bacteria from invading and damaging the intestinal tract. A leaky gut can lead to increased susceptibility to food allergies and problems in learning, behavior, and overall health.

After starting Brian on a natural antifungal and probiotics, we noticed a dramatic improvement. Brian was definitely more alert and began imitating everything. His eyes had complete clarity and he seemed more connected than ever before. Because of this response we decided to be more aggressive with a prescription antifungal. We also wanted to check the aluminum and nutrient levels again.

We went to Dr. Warren Levin, M.D., a specialist in natural or complementary medicine. After running comprehensive blood, stool, and urine tests, the results indicated that Brian had a leaky gut and that candida was still present. He continued to be deficient in certain nutrients, most notably, the B vitamins. We increased his doses of B6 and magnesium and added several other supplements. We identified other foods that were problematic for Brian and eliminated these from his diet.

Brian received his second infusion of secretin with no noticeable changes. While these therapies may have been inconvenient, to say the least, Brian had not been developing without them. With them, he was thriving and closing the gap in his delays. Brian was making remarkable progress.

One year after Brian's diagnosis, he showed incredible gains across the board. His new Birth to Three evaluation showed gains in language from a three-month level a year ago to an eighteen- to twenty-month level. His personal social scores jumped from a five-month level to twenty months and his fine and gross motor skills jumped from a thirteen-month level to age appropriate.

When Brian received a third infusion of secretin, we noted an increase in both his receptive and expressive language. We were encouraged by this and called to schedule another infusion. We indicated that Brian was scheduled for AIT and were advised that secretin could potentially reverse its effects. We decided not to give Brian any additional infusions of secretin until we saw how he responded to AIT.

Brian received AIT a month before his third birthday. A friend of mine had arranged for an AIT practitioner, Jackie Rockwell, to come to New Jersey to conduct a session. We stayed at my parents' house while Brian received his twenty sessions of AIT over ten days. I wasn't sure how we'd get Brian to wear the required headphones. While his severe reaction to familiar people had diminished, he was still apprehensive about unfamiliar people and places. Transitions remained difficult for him and I wasn't sure how these ten days would go.

The first morning, when we went into the hotel suite, Brian was definitely anxious. When we put the headphones on him he started to scream and thrash about and tried to pull them off. I had to hold him on my lap while restraining him. Jackie held the headphones on so that they wouldn't come off as he shook his head desperately trying to remove them. This went on for almost the entire first thirty-minute session. He didn't have strong enough language skills to understand what was happening. After the first session he knew that he only had to listen to the music. Maybe he even enjoyed it because when we returned that afternoon, Brian readily accepted the headphones and relaxed on my lap. He some-times grew restless but we had no problem keeping the head-phones on for the remainder of the sessions.

The changes became apparent during the ten days of therapy. While Brian had been using two-to-three-word prompted phrases, he was now using five-to-six-word *spontaneous* phrases. He would arrive at the hotel and look for the front desk people to say hello to. He got up one morning and said, "Hi Grandpa," for the first time on his own initiative. Instead of plunking himself down in the tub as if it had no temperature, he put his foot in, removed it, and commented, "Ooh, it's hot." He had never appeared to notice the temperature, let alone comment on it. "Hot" was also an abstract thought that he didn't seem to understand before. When we went to a carpet store, instead of his usual clinging to me and getting upset, he left me and followed the salesman around, trying to talk to him.

When we got back to Connecticut, his therapists were amazed. Even though he had missed almost two weeks of ABA, he had made remarkable gains. They told us that they had not expected much from the AIT but that its effects on Brian were undeniable. Brian was a different child. He was able to answer questions and have simple conversation. He noticed and commented on sounds that had been part of his everyday environment as if he were hearing them for the first time. He was spontaneous and interested in everyone and everything. Driving in the car, he named everything he saw as if to say, "See, Mom, I know what it is. I just couldn't tell you before."

A huge breakthrough in his ability to communicate occurred when we went for a haircut the week he finished AIT. Haircuts had always been terribly traumatic for him and we were never exactly sure why. We didn't know if it was the sound of the scissors, the lighting, or something else that was so upsetting to him. After AIT, during the haircut he pointed to a tiny piece of hair on his arm and said, "Ow." I now knew that he actually had physical discomfort from the hair on his skin. Haircuts became easier when we knew to cover all his skin and make the hair heavier by getting it very wet. The feather-light touch of dry hair probably felt like razors cutting him but he could never tell me it hurt before. It's the same reason Brian cried on sand and hated to be in the grass even with shoes on. It hurt him.

Two weeks after AIT we moved to New Jersey. Brian was turning three and we did not feel our school district in Connecticut could meet his needs. We had also checked out several other programs in Connecticut, New York, and North Jersey. Many of the behaviorally based schools did not address or acknowledge as legitimate the sensory and nutritional issues that we felt were the basis of Brian's autism. We went to one private school that consisted of one room with fourteen tables and chairs. The children literally sat back to back while trying to process and respond to six hundred to a thousand commands in a six-hour day. They were given foods containing gluten, casein, and sugar continuously as reinforcers. The only break area was at the opposite end of the same room where they ate lunch, or in the center of the room for some floor time. They did not get any exercise and had no speech or occupational therapy, no art or other sensory stimulating or desensitizing play. How distracting this room was.

I left and cried the whole way home and told my husband they could give me the $58,000 tuition and they still couldn't have my child! The local school district was willing to work with us and establish a program including direct teaching and discrete trials. However, they were going to put him in a small audiovisual storage closet to do it and learn as they went. It may have been nobler to stay and help them create a program but we needed to put Brian's needs first. We wanted to go where they already knew what he needed and were equipped to provide it.

Mark explained to his human resource department that our son had special needs and that some of the best programs for

autism were in New Jersey. Within days he was given the opportunity to interview with a division of his company in Pennsylvania,
close to the New Jersey line. Many of the more notable schools in
New Jersey, like Eden and Princeton Child Development Institute
(PCDI), had long waiting lists. As we began to second-guess our
decision, I once again prayed for direction. I opened a book listing public and private autism programs to a page listing a county
sponsored program in Trenton, New Jersey. I was hesitant to call
when even some private schools in exclusive areas did not meet our
satisfaction.

The principal was amazing, rearranging her schedule to meet
with me the next day. The school was bright and airy with a gym-
nasium and therapy rooms for occupational and physical therapies.
There was a cafeteria for children who could handle eating lunch
in a large room. Artwork made by the children hung outside every
classroom. The staff was enthusiastic and you could see the difference on the children's faces compared to those we had seen elsewhere. They had a two-to-one student-teacher ratio with no more
than six children in a classroom. A full-day, year around program
was designed specifically to meet the needs of children with
autism. Brian would receive speech therapy five days a week. It was
everything we could have hoped for.

After crying and hugging the principal who had to think I
was nuts, I got into my car and called my husband. I told him to
accept the job transfer because Brian was going to Joseph Cappello
School. I met a realtor and bought a house that day in a district
that would refer Brian to the school.

When we brought Brian in to Cappello for his evaluation,
the child we brought with us didn't match the evaluations from
only three months before as Brian had received AIT the month
before we moved to New Jersey. Mark and I remained with him

and he did not exhibit any anxiety. He was social and engaged and had no trouble completing his tasks. While he was still a child with multiple delays and sensory integration issues consistent with his autism diagnosis, the evaluators remarked that he did not present himself as a child with autism. Mark and I, who knew his every ability and skill from his home program, noted that he was doing things and behaving in a way that had not been possible only weeks before.

Among those who didn't know Brian before he received AIT, there is still skepticism regarding the role it, as well as the other complementary therapies Brian has received, has played in his recovery. There is no doubt in my mind, or in the minds of those who knew and worked with Brian from the beginning, that AIT helped him dramatically. Before AIT, the world of hypersensitive hearing was too painful to tune in to. I'm convinced that much of what we said to Brian was not processed properly and therefore made little sense to him. Without a doubt, I know that AIT and the nutritional therapies we have used to treat Brian enabled him to open up and be receptive to his teachers. As his ABA tutor, Audra, always said, the most important thing is that he is engaged and available to learn. Without these combined therapies I am certain Brian would not have progressed this far, this quickly, if at all.

Even though there is no guarantee that AIT will help, or that AIT and other therapies will help all children to the same extent, the very fact that they have helped thousands worldwide for decades makes it irresponsible not to try them. There is enough research and scientific data to support the validity of each of these interventions. I've always known that I never wanted to look back and think that I didn't do everything I could to help Brian reach his potential. Even if he remained autistic but simply felt better or had less painful hearing, our efforts would have been justified.

Over the past five years I have come across doctors and educators, some well-meaning and others too arrogant to open their minds to what parents are telling them, who have dismissed and discouraged other parents from trying any treatments other than mainstream medicine. The ironic thing about this is that mainstream medicine doesn't offer any treatment and can't offer any stories of children recovering from autism.

I had a discussion once at my son's school with a teacher I liked and respected. She could not understand how parents could choose gluten/casein free-diets or any other nonbehavioral interventions for their child. She, like so many others, assumed that one had to make a choice between ABA and other therapies. I explained that there is not a choice of one to the exclusion of the other. The nonbehavioral interventions actually complement the behavioral. I used an analogy of eyeglasses. If your child cannot see clearly, you get him glasses. Without them it doesn't matter how great his teacher or school program is, he's never going to see clearly until you get glasses for him. You do not choose between the two. You still need a strong and appropriate educational program. It's just easier to learn when you can see clearly. That's what AIT and other therapies do. They help your child see, hear and feel better.

Another thing that people forget is that people with autism have nutritional, digestive, and immunological problems. Kids with autism also have sensory integration issues. How can any teacher help children reach their potential when they don't feel well or can't focus because they are trying to process or block out the sights, sounds, and smells in their environment? They can't!

Soon after moving to New Jersey, I attended my second DAN! Conference, where I met Maribeth Mydlowski, a local chiropractor and Naet practitioner. Naet is an allergy elimination treatment, which combines aspects of applied kinesiology, chiropractic, and acupressure to eliminate sensitivity to food or other environmental allergens. I took Brian and Meghan to Dr. Mydlowski and we followed her protocol to eliminate sensitivity to a series of foods and chemicals that are added to our food everyday. I read up on this (see http://www.naet.com) and decided that, although the effects might not be obvious, Naet would benefit both children.

I didn't expect any noticeable improvements in Meghan as she is developing typically with no delays or behaviors. Even Brian, at that point, had no significant communication or behavioral issues. It's as if you're already on the second floor of a tall building and you go to the first. The view is not much different. It's when you go from the basement to the second floor that the improvements are remarkable. I mention this, as Naet is a viable and effective therapy. Conventional blood tests and EEGs have shown it to be helpful in reducing symptoms of allergy-related autism. It is described in Dr. William Shaw's new must-read book, *Biological Treatments for Autism and PDD.*

We repeated blood, stool, and urine tests while working with Maureen McDonnell, R.N., who has an office in Pennington, New Jersey. She consults with Dr. Sidney Baker on test results and he prescribed another antifungal and a sugar-and-yeast-free diet in our continuing effort to rid Brian of candida. These attempts were successful and he has been able to maintain a healthy intestinal environment.

Brian was doing so well that we discussed the idea of putting our feet up and allowing Brian to continue his development without pursuing any additional therapies. Of course, we would continue his gluten/casein-free diet, nutritional supplements, and chiropractic care. Understanding our desire to leave no stone unturned and bring Brian to optimal health and functioning, Maureen suggested that we make sure that there were no toxic metals, such as mercury, in his body. She referred us to Dr. James Neubrander for chelation therapy. As stated in the *Autism Research Review International,* Volume 17, No. 1, a new study "provides strong epidemiological evidence for a link between mercury exposure from thimerosal-containing childhood vaccines and neurodevelopment disorders." "Instantaneous mercury levels in children receiving thimerosal-containing vaccines exceeded EPA standards by up to 150-fold and FDA guidelines by up to 37-fold." It has been suggested by doctors such as Amy Holmes, M.D., that the current epidemic of autism has been caused by mercury poisoning from childhood vaccines, the symptoms of which are almost identical to autistic symptoms.

Brian underwent chelation therapy to remove the low level of toxic mercury that was confirmed through provoking tests. Mercury is not always apparent in a typical blood test unless the exposure was within weeks of the test. This is because mercury, as Dr. Neubrander described it, is like a lobster that grabs on to your bones and brain tissue and doesn't let go unless forced to with a chelating agent, such as dimercaptosuccinic acid (DMSA). Other products are also being used for detoxification such as L-Glutathione and thamine tetrahydrofurfurl disulfide (TTFD). These were discussed at the most recent DAN! Conference in Philadelphia. No level of mercury is acceptable so we followed his protocol for its removal. Dr. Neubrander is also having great success with Methl-B12 shots. Parents are noting great improvement in their child's speech and behavior with these therapies.

Brian remained at Joseph Cappello school for two years. It was an amazing experience for him. The first year, Jodi, his teacher, took him under her wing and helped him feel safe. Even when she was no longer his teacher, Brian would spot her in the hallway before she even noticed him and yell, "I love you, Jodi!" Not what you would typically expect in a school full of autistic children. They were completely supportive of his diet and other therapies. In fact, one day I walked into his classroom and saw that his teacher had a book on the diet. His individual education program (IEP) specifies that he only be given food that has been sent from home or has been specifically approved by me. They always keep a supply of frozen treats at school for parties and special occasions that have been approved by the parents. This support is essential.

His second year at Cappello was geared specifically to preparing Brian and four other high-functioning children for transition back to district schools and a mainstream kindergarten. Sharon, his teacher, was one of the most enthusiastic and gifted teachers we have ever known.

He turned five only weeks before he began kindergarten. This is amazing when you consider how delayed he was when he was diagnosed just a few months before his second birthday. He went off on a bus with his sister and the other neighborhood kids for the first time. Although I had known for a while that he would be okay, my emotions caught me by surprise and I cried like a baby.

In a collaborative kindergarten class taught by one regular education teacher and one special education teacher, he was one of sixteen children, eleven of whom were "typical." He did wonderfully. Much of the credit for his successful transition to the mainstream was due to the high caliber of his teachers and the appropriate level of support he received. He had speech, occupational therapy, and resource room alternatively each afternoon when the typical kids went home after a half-day. By his sixth birthday he no longer required an extended school year and was ready for a mainstream first grade class with one regular education teacher and nineteen children.

He is mainstreamed for the majority of the day, but is pulled into the resource room for math, reading, and language arts. He requires speech therapy once a week that focuses on auditory processing and auditory memory. No one who meets Brian suspects his history and a classmate's mom just asked me yesterday why he is pulled out of class at all. Brian is very bright and follows the same curriculum as the rest of his class. However, he is distracted easily. We believe that this is due, in part, to his highly social and outgoing nature. I'm sure that it is also due, in part, to his residual sound sensitivity. As he recently described it, the mainstream class "sounds like everyone is yelling all the time but I know they're not." The small group helps to limit these distractions. Once again, he is extremely fortunate to have an excellent team of teachers and the appropriate level of support.

We have arranged that Sally Brockett come to New Jersey this summer to conduct an AIT session for a group of children, including Brian. We hope that this "fine-tuning" of Brian's hearing will help reduce or eliminate his sound sensitivity and distractibility.

Brian's miracle of recovery has taken time, but it has been worth it. He is a happy, well-adjusted little boy. As his sister has said, "he is very popular" and his teachers have all confirmed that he is a class favorite with the other children. His interests are varied and "appropriate." He played Pop Warner Football last fall and basketball this past winter. He began karate five months ago and we do not even have to mention his history to his coaches and instructors. He will be in a local theatre camp production this summer. He's just one of the kids.

In sharp contrast to what we were told the day he was diagnosed, Brian can achieve anything he wants in life. He is an adorable little boy, a real charmer who steals the hearts of all who know him. He has a sense of humor and wants to be a part of everything. He makes friends wherever he goes and has better verbal and social skills than most children his age.

Although at one time our entire focus was on helping Brian get well, our lives are typical now. Sure, Brian continues to take vitamins, but so do we all. He goes to Dr. Caskey twice a year, but so do we all. He has to avoid certain foods, but many people deal with food allergies. He gets pulled out of class for special help in a couple of subjects in school, but so do a lot of kids. Brian does not act differently than other children and they do not see him as any different.

The road to recovery for Brian has been difficult. However, it has been filled with many blessings too. Through every accomplishment we have experienced great joy. We take nothing Brian says or does for granted. There have been many people who have come into our lives that we would not have otherwise met. They are the angels God sent to do His work. We have gotten our miracle, one day at a time.

I learned to lean on others while always trusting my instincts. I knew that I knew my child better than anyone. I didn't give up or turn back but kept moving forward and keep moving forward. When I felt lost or discouraged, I thought of the familiar story of "Footprints in the Sand" by Margaret Fishback Powers:

> One night a man had a dream. He dreamed he was walking along the beach with the Lord. Across the sky flashed scenes from his life. For each scene, he noticed two sets of footprints in the sand; one belonging to

him, the other to the Lord. When the last scene of his life flashed before him, he looked back at the footprints in the sand. He noticed that many times along the path of his life there was only one set of footprints. He also noticed that it happened at the very lowest and saddest times in his life. This really bothered him and he questioned the Lord about it. "Lord, you said that once I decided to follow you, you'd walk with me all the way. But I have noticed that during the most troublesome times in my life, there is only one set of footprints. I don't understand why when I needed you most you would leave me." The Lord replied, "My precious, precious child, I love you and would never leave you. During your times of trial and suffering, when you see only one set of footprints, it was then that I carried you."

KEEGAN

Sheila Clancy

Keegan was diagnosed with sensory integration dysfunction at age five, and I remember getting that diagnosis, reading Carol Stock Kranowitz's *The Out-of-Sync-Child*, and feeling as if someone had thrown us a lifeline. We were finally beginning to understand our son and all his eccentricities. Later, through continued work with developmental pediatricians, neurologists, occupational therapists, and all the other myriad of experts we saw, he was diagnosed with Asperger's syndrome.

Asperger Syndrome or Asperger's Disorder is a neurobiological disorder named for a Viennese physician, Hans Asperger, who in 1944 published a paper which described a pattern of behaviors in several young boys who had normal intelligence and language development, but who also exhibited autistic-like behaviors and marked deficiencies in social and communication skills.

I wish you could know him, as he is a pure delight. He is such a unique little guy, and very much the little professor "aspies" are often described as. Many of his "sensory issues" have dissipated in the last two years, but none as quickly or dramatically as the sound sensitivities after auditory integration training (AIT).

Prior to AIT, Keegan was terrified (terror doesn't even come close to describing the depth of his fear) of so many normal sounds: hair dryers, vacuum cleaners, airplanes, lawnmowers, smoke alarms, fire alarms, etc. Our days were full of conversations of "What's that noise?" and me saying "What noise, I don't hear anything." I would have to really listen to try to pinpoint the noise he was hearing. Often it was a very faint, to me: a lawnmower blocks away, or an airplane so far in the distance that I could barely detect it.

When he was younger, about three or four, he would ask everyone, as soon as he arrived at their house, where their vacuum cleaner was. He wanted to know exactly where it was kept, and if he saw anyone headed in that direction, he would hightail it out of the house.

We consulted our pediatrician about it at the time and got a very pat, "it's a phase" answer. Later, after he had gotten tubes in his ears and the fears and aversions to noise continued, we were told it was because he was hearing sounds as they actually sounded for the first time and would need some time to adjust. In the interim, Keegan refused to enter public restrooms that had hand dryers. He would make me check first and if they had "just paper towels" we could go in. He also wouldn't enter his preschool if he saw the garage doors open . . . this meant that they would be cutting the grass with the riding lawn movers. We made so many adjustments . . . no vacuuming while he was home, no hair drying, using the blender, etc. When there was a fire drill at school, he would absolutely shut down. He had to be carried out of the building and it would take days to calm him down.

Last spring my father consulted a medical library in Wilmington, Delaware, looking for information on autism. This alone is a miracle. In the thirty-five years that I have known my father, I have never seen him read a book or enter a library. I know he had to do some research to find out where to go, and inquire about what he wanted once he got there. He is a sixty-nine-year-old man who has never used a computer or microfilm or probably even a card catalog in his life. But among the books he came home with was *Sound of a Miracle*. I had read a brief description of AIT on the Schafer Autism calendar, a calendar of events relating to autism published by the *Schafer Autism Report*, whose mission is to promote autism awareness and education toward finding the best treatments, preventions, and cures for a range of disorders labeled as the "autism spectrum." But I had little grasp of what it entailed. Once I read this book, I knew it was something we had to try for Keegan.

Our treatment philosophy for him has pretty much been to try anything that may help, so long as it can't hurt. I honestly felt that my father finding this book was a sign that this was the right thing to do and the right time to try it. I called Terrie Silverman and filled one of the last slots in her AIT program in Philadelphia, about forty-five minutes from my parents' home.

So Keegan and I went to spend ten days with my parents. It wasn't the easiest or the most inexpensive of days. But the rewards were priceless. I would have to find my journal and revisit precisely the exact days on which things occurred, but I know that on about day five he started sleeping through the night. This was a first for us . . . and after six years an unbelievable blessing! He used to wake up a few times a night with, "I heard something scary," and now it was me waking up wondering why he wasn't waking up!

I think it was about the same time that we returned home

one evening from our sessions and my dad was driving up the driveway on his tractor (they live on a farm and I know he was doing the mowing while Keegan was away as the tractor is very loud). Keegan waved and said, "Hi, Papa Joe." I didn't think anything of it at first, and then realized he was still standing next to me, holding my hand and looking, and talking to my dad while the tractor was still running. My dad and I just looked at each other in awe. Then my dad asked, "Would you like to go for a ride with me?" Keegan, with no hesitation, said, "okay," and climbed up to my dad's lap. I just stood there in amazement and cried. He climbed up there with no trepidation, no anxiety, just the sheer joy of a grandchild riding and steering a big green tractor while sitting on his granddad's lap.

I asked him about it later when we got home to Richmond, and he told me, "My ears don't feel like they're going to explode anymore and my head doesn't feel like it has a disease."

We were outside a few days later and he looked up, pointed and said, "Hey, Mom, cool, an airplane," and went back to playing. Again I was shocked. Normally, he would have run inside so fast at the first sound of the airplane and refused to come back out. Now he really barely noticed. We continued to see such huge changes, things I wouldn't have thought to look for. He went swimming for the first time. He has always been terrified of water splashing on him, and now he was wading in water chest high, and rode bumper boats with squirt guns and got soaking wet. He was laughing, squealing, and having so much fun, I could not believe my eyes. As my mother and best friend both commented, "He just seems so much more comfortable in his own skin."

He began to respond and follow multi-step directions. When I asked him to go up, put his pajamas on, brush his teeth, and put his clothes in the hamper, he actually did all four things the first time I asked. We had a very successful Kindergarten year with Keegan receiving the most improved academically award. He is a different child after AIT. He can enjoy fireworks. I never thought I would write that!

Keegan's previous teacher conferences were huge anxiety producers for me. We heard lots of, "We can't meet his needs," "He is in his own little world," "He has trouble listening and focusing," and many, many more discouraging remarks. He attended a small private kindergarten this year and his teacher asked me, "Are you sure he has Asperger's?" She told me repeatedly that she didn't see any of the issues I had described. Below is a sample of his national percentile rank scores on the Iowa test of basic skills.

- Vocabulary (listening vocabulary): 94th percentile
- Word Analysis (how well students recognize letters and letter/sound relationships): 83rd percentile
- Listening (short oral scenarios presented and then questions read. Testsability to follow directions, understand sequences, and predict outcomes): 82nd percentile
- Language (ability to understand linguistic relationships — how language is used to express ideas): 97th percentile

Prior to AIT, and prior to admittance to the private school, he took an IQ test that showed a huge discrepancy between verbal and performance IQ, and the school was not willing to admit him. I begged, and the school agreed to take him on a trial basis only, with no guarantee he would be allowed to stay for the full year. I look at those scores now and think, how is it possible that this is the same child?

All I can say is I know Keegan would not be the child he is

now without AIT. Even if the only benefit we received was that he was able to sleep through the night, it would have been well worth it, but the benefits have been so much more. As Keegan says, "I think that listening stuff really helped."

MICHAEL

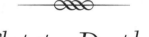

Christine Davidson

My son, Michael, was born very healthy. Although his rubella "titers" (A "titer" is a measurement of how much antibody to a certain virus, or other antigen, is circulating in the blood at that moment.) were high. Some say that's normal, some say it's not. It may have had something to do with the fact that he changed after his first-year inoculations. He lost his speech, his eye contact, and his desire to interact in and discover the world in a normally developing way.

We began a course of repeated infusions of gamma globulin given intravenously to boost his primary immune system. Nutritional healing of the intestinal lining is a slow, methodical process, and this was a key element in the healing of his primary immune system. His nutritional needs were met by trial and error. Concoctions of vitamins, minerals, and especially chlorophyll worked to provide a new balance. It took many years of balancing and counterbalancing modalities. Sensory integration therapy,

speech and language therapy, behavior patterning for speech and
learned interaction, and a young boy's desire to achieve, to be successful, were all contributing factors. Most influential of all was
auditory integration training (AIT) when Michael was three years
old. It was something simple, alternative, and precise. And it
worked . . . it worked! Like a magic wand, AIT allowed his young
brain to heal. Without it, without eliminating the pain of hyperacute and distorted hearing, nothing would have mattered. In our
bodies lies an understanding that, in order to receive treatment of
any kind, the host, our body, our immunity, our physical state of
being, must first be balanced. That is exactly what AIT did. It created the opportunity to heal. It created the miracle we so desperately needed.

We could see Michael improve with immune therapy and
diet changes, his recovery slowly waxing and waning until it eventually ironed itself out. As the blood tests showed his rubella levels going down, his primary immune system was strengthening. Yet
the behavioral progress could only go so far. Soft, almost inaudible sounds caused him excruciating pain. Pervasive mental confusion was affecting his ability to interact. Most heart wrenching was
to watch this beautiful little boy trying to play and laugh, only
to stop in his tracks and cry because of pains in his head.

—∞—

Like a bolt from the blue, my prayers were answered through
a newsletter that recounted the success of children who had gone
through AIT therapy. I did not know that, at that moment, my life
was truly to begin again. The opportunity, and the eventual
cure, were already in motion, but all I knew in that summer of
1992 was that I was simply excited to be going to Canada to try a
new therapy. When Michael received his AIT, he was participating

in his treatment and was clearly affected. He was sleepier than usual on some days, and overly restless on others, all to be expected. Then it happened.

As we stood at the window overlooking the bay in beautiful Victoria, British Columbia, watching the scheduled ferryboat arrive, Michael spoke his first words. "I hear boat," he said. Words. Real words, expressive words, magnificent sounds from our three-year-old's mouth. They were soft yet distinct, and in that moment, hope ingrained itself and we as parents knew, looking with amazement, that eventually Michael would be okay. He was not at that moment, but eventually he would be.

Jubilantly, we took days off to explore the surroundings, ride the ferries, swim in the ocean, and feed the seagulls at the shoreline. All of a sudden, wonderful, normal activity was possible. Michael was not bothered by sounds anymore. He was happy and no longer in pain, and from that time on, he was never in pain again.

Months of therapies followed, years of positive reinforcement, daily rituals of nutrition and supplements that eventually paid off. Regular school, regular teachers, and regular sports and activities filled his life.

Years later, in fourth grade, Michael participated in a "Fast ForWord" auditory program made available through speech pathologists. Fast ForWord further enchanced his brain's ability to recognize sounds and improve his auditory processing.

In elementary school he received quality instruction, eventually scoring so high as to no longer qualify for special education resources. As an eighth grader in junior high, he made honor roll and was chosen to be student of the month. Today, Michael is a normal, healthy, tall young man entering high school with no memories of the pain and suffering of his childhood. He remembers his teachers, he understands his past, and he recognizes his example of hope to others.

His interests are creative and artistic as well as academic. He is a talented writer and a very good filmmaker, especially adept at computer-generated special effects. He is compassionate and kind and carries himself with diplomatic style and grace. He is my perfect son, just the way God created him to be. And this all became possible because of one woman's courage. Thank you, Annabel Stehli, for my son and my life.

ANDY AND BRYAN

---◦◦◦---

Barbara Townsend

INTRODUCTION

My husband Ron and I met in 1981 in the office of a small consulting firm near New York City. We were close friends for seven
years and finally married in 1988. He was 34 and I was 29. Our
backgrounds were similar. We were both of English descent, we
each had two siblings all close in age, our families were well-edu-
cated, we both had majored in mathematics in college, and we had
the same deep religious roots. We were well-off financially when
we were married since we had both worked and saved since college.

We wanted a big family and immediately bought a house in
an upper-middle-class town in central New Jersey known to have
an excellent school system (little did we know how important that
would be). Nine months later our first son, Gary, was born. He
was the first grandchild on my side and the long-awaited grandchild on Ron's side as they were starting to wonder if he would
ever marry. Gary was absolutely adorable, a blue-eyed towhead. He

was loved to death, and he was normal, a fact that I took totally for granted. Life was perfect. Andy followed two-and-a-half years later, then Bryan twenty-one months after that, and finally Scott almost three years after Bryan. The pregnancies, births, and even birthweights (around eight pounds) were nearly identical. They were all breastfed for the first six months. Andy and Bryan are autistic. These are their stories.

ANDY

Ron and I wanted our first two children to be very close in age, so when I became pregnant when Gary was about seven months old, we were thrilled. I had a miscarriage two weeks later and was told to just wait a month and try again. After three months I was starting to panic. It was so easy before — what happened? Finally, after a year of testing both of us to varying degrees (and considerable expense), I became pregnant with Andy. The testing was all at my insistence as any doctor worth his salt will tell you that you have to try for at least three years before you're considered an infertility problem. I told them I didn't have that kind of time and just *do* something. I'm still quite friendly with my gynecologist — I think he liked my tenacity. Anyway, the only reason I bring this up is because down the road we were questioned as to whether or not, deep down, we had really wanted this child!

Andy was a wonderful baby. He was blond and chubby with huge blue eyes and long black eyelashes (later, a pediatric neurologist would tell me that many of the children he saw with food allergies had exceptionally long lashes). He slept through the night from day one, ate well, progressed well physically, and rarely cried. He was happy to be carried around in his car seat or in anyone's arms for that matter. He turned over in his crib at four months — once. He never turned over again. It was as if he was thinking, okay, I tried it and it was no big deal — I'm happy the way I am. By seven months he sat, stood against a table, and roamed in his walker if you put him in those positions. He never made an attempt to do these things himself. He seemed happy wherever and however you put him. He never crawled. Years later, I discovered that this is a necessary stage of development. For me, though, he was a dream child, as I was still dealing with Gary who was an active, very verbal toddler — a real handful.

Andy walked on his eleven-month birthday. He simply turned away from the table and walked away. He wasn't interested in accolades. There was little or no babbling and certainly no words. I saw him as the shy type, as I had always been. I felt as though I thoroughly understood him, and the idea that there may be a problem never crossed my mind. Gary loved Andy (and vice versa) and they would horse around together in his crib and in the playpen. I didn't think it was unusual that Andy never initiated the play (even a year later) since Gary was the older and more gregarious of the two boys.

As a young toddler, Andy often had a runny nose (clear, not green). I questioned my pediatrician about allergies, especially since Ron had bad allergies, and they are often inherited. The doctor said Andy was too young. He would always check Andy's ears and throat and although he would sometimes see redness and fluid, he rarely prescribed antibiotics. I'm grateful for this now, although I was not at the time, since massive doses of antibiotics have been associated with autism. (An aside about my pediatrician, Dr. Taylor: He is a gifted physician, but doesn't like to talk. He's very shy. In the fifteen years that I've known him, maybe we've had five conversations. After leaving him for about four years in search of a doctor who would help me fight autism, I finally figured out that I knew more than any doctor, but if one of my children had cancer or something equally as horrible, Dr. Taylor is the only one I'd want them with. We've come full circle and now have a mutual respect for each other.) So, except for his chronic runny nose, Andy was healthy, although at eleven months he had the worst case of roseola I've ever seen (a fever that hovered around 105 for two days — we ended up in the emergency room because nothing would bring it down) and at nineteen months he had the worst case of chicken pox I've ever seen. He couldn't wear clothes, not even a diaper. Through it all, he didn't really cry or complain in any way. Although I don't think these sicknesses caused his developmental problems, I do think the severity of them is proof positive that autistic children have compromised immune systems.

The very first inkling that I had that there was cause for concern came when Andy was seventeen months old. I was working in the office three days a week and would bring the boys to my mother's house where she and my grandmother cared for them. They loved it there (and still do). Gary particularly liked to help his great-grandmother cook. My mother was a seamstress at that time. The iron was always turned on and sitting on the ironing board which was right at Andy's height. Although she was very careful and kept the door shut, Andy could maneuver around like a quiet little tornado and, sure enough, the iron landed on top of his right hand. Since he had a bad burn, I was in Dr. Taylor's office every other day for two weeks having it cleaned, bandaged, and checked. It was during these visits that the doctor was forced to make idle chitchat. "So, I assume he's talking." "No, he's not." "Surely he says mama or dada?" "NO, nothing." [Over the next two years I must have said this a hundred times.] The look of concern on his face scared me. I never forgot it. "Does he understand you?" "I'm not sure." "Does he make his needs known?" "Yes."

I thought to myself that he only had two "needs" — that he

wanted orange juice or to watch his favorite videotape. He would drag a chair to the refrigerator, get out the juice, and plop it in my lap. Since he slept with the videotape and knew where it was at all times, he would bring it to one of us to insert. It was a happy day when, two years later, he figured out how to work the VCR himself.

My answers seemed to placate Dr. Taylor. He said that he's a boy, he's the second child, and Gary probably does most of his talking for him. He probably just has a processing problem. So when I left, Dr. Taylor was happy and I was just beginning to realize that I was starting on the toughest journey of my life. Although my mother still cringes with guilt every time she sees Andy's scar, I tell her I always see it as a blessing.

Bryan was born shortly thereafter, and I decided I would take the summer off and relax with the new baby and observe Andy more closely, and that I would call the nearby child development center, which had a wonderful reputation, in September armed with my observations. Besides his complete lack of speech, except for rare grunting sounds that specialists would later call *back vocal* or *vowel sounds*, Andy appeared, to the casual observer, to be deaf. He did not respond to his name or any type of instruction. However, if I put on his favorite videotape — it was a Disney sing-along tape where the words flashed along the bottom of the screen — he appeared from the farthest corner of the house in twenty seconds or less.

He was very quick and agile and more coordinated than a toddler should be. He also had an uncanny sense of balance. When he ran, though, he never looked straight ahead; rather he looked down to his left side as if he were watching an invisible line. We were always amazed that he never once bumped into anything. He thought nothing of walking in the snow and ice with bare feet.

He didn't seem to notice the sensation of cold.

His play was extremely limited. He would lie on the floor with his left ear to the ground, squint, and roll a truck or train (it didn't matter what the toy was as long as it had at least two wheels that were perfectly aligned) back and forth in front of his eyes — three inches beyond and three inches below. You could leave him there for hours and go shopping, and he never noticed you were gone. I thought he was a genius.

Andy was never violent; in fact, quite the opposite. He was very meek. He rarely, if ever, head-banged, toe-walked, or hit or bit himself or others. In all the years he's been in school, he only bit two children while on the playground. My guess is that they deserved it. When he was extremely frustrated, he would scream and shake and go to bite his arm or fist but at the last second would bite his sleeve instead. These episodes increased as he got older, which was probably a good thing as it showed that he cared about *something*, although it wasn't pleasant at the time. His eye contact with me was fairly good, slightly less with other family members, and virtually nonexistent with anyone else. He had no interest in other children (which worked out well for me because I had no interest in their moms). Besides, it became too painful for me to watch him around normal kids.

His favorite foods were pasta, cereal, and orange juice. He also had three bottles of whole milk per day, one of which contained his vitamins since he wouldn't take them alone. I eliminated dairy products for a time after reading Doris Rapp's book about food allergies, but there was no change, so we went back to the milk. None of this seemed abnormal to me — this is what most kids his age ate. The problem today is that this is *still* all he'll eat. He seems to have a problem with the texture of many types of foods — he physically gags on meat. Over the years, this has been a problem with extended family meals. I love the maxim "If you leave it there long enough, he'll eat it. He won't starve." Wrong! An autistic child would far prefer to starve.

On September 1, the day after Andy's second birthday, I called the child development center with a tremendous amount of anticipation. I was going to help my child (who I never thought was much different from me). After being put on hold several times, I got a human who asked me questions for at least forty-five minutes. "When did he roll over, crawl, walk, talk, etc.?" "He never talked, that's why I'm calling." I was finally told that there was a waiting list of six to eight months. [You couldn't have told me that in the first place?] I put Andy on the list.

I hung up in a panic and called my mother and Ron. I assumed that when I was ready to really dig in and help Andy, I could snap my fingers and it would happen. Boy, was I wrong, and I never made that mistake again. They suggested I call my sister, a physician. She pulled some strings and got an appointment a month later with a neurodevelopmental pediatrician at University Hospital in Newark. She felt that he had serious language and social delays, but otherwise he was normal. She suggested speech therapy and even agreed to contact the developmental center that had turned me away. I was relieved.

Within a week we were "accepted" at the development center for speech services only — two sessions a week for a half-hour each. The speech therapist was a nice enough young woman who seemed to know her stuff. She would strap Andy into a little wooden chair (since he wouldn't stay on his own), force him to make eye contact, and try to teach him a few "functional" words, as she put it. ["Please" and "thank you" were not functional words — we had to stay away from them. Wrong! They were the first words I taught him. If he was going to go through life with disabilities, he was at least going to be polite about it.] He hated these sessions. He would cry, scream, and kick. She finally had to tie his feet to the chair. Needless to say, no words were forthcoming.

At the same time, my mother-in-law was doing some networking of her own. A good friend of hers had been on the staff of Boston Children's Hospital prior to his retirement years earlier. Amazingly, he made three appointments for us over a two-day period on November 2 and 3. Never having met Andy and knowing only that Andy did not speak, he made appointments with an audiologist, a speech therapist, and an ear, nose, and throat specialist (ENT). This proved to be one of many turning points in the process. All three specialists were brilliant, gentle, caring women. The audiologist felt that Andy had sufficient hearing within normal tones to have developed some language. How she figured this out is still a mystery to me. She could tell certain things simply by the flutter of his eyelashes!

That afternoon we visited with the speech therapist. She spent two hours with him even though it was his regular naptime and he was not at his best. She was actually able to engage him, at least for short periods of time. She felt that he had some symptoms of pervasive developmental delay (PDD), but she presented this information in a positive way, and provided us with a list of things to do at home to promote the desire to speak. Without meaningful play and good imitation skills, language was unlikely to develop. She also wanted us to make an appointment with the hospital's clinical psychologist, which we did for November 23. There is usually a six month to a year wait to get in, but there had been a cancellation. God was watching over us again!

The visit with the ENT the next morning was enlightening, to say the least. Andy had fluid in his ears that was amber colored, which meant that it had been there a long time. This could have impeded speech development. She recommended a myringotomy (tubes in both ears) and an adenoidectomy. We were able to schedule the surgery in Boston for the following week. The five-hour drive was never an issue with us. We loved this place.

The early morning surgery went well, and by midafternoon, Ron, Andy, and I were back in our hotel room where Andy slept. By dinnertime, he seemed to have fully recovered, and we were actually noticing small changes in him. He smiled more and he seemed to try to talk (meaning his back vocal grunts were louder and more expressive). Although Andy still did not speak for at least two more years, we feel that his hearing had to be at its absolute optimum level. To us, the surgery was a success. It was one step up the ladder toward normalcy and the adenoidectomy seemed to clear up his runny nose.

Two weeks later, it was back to Boston to meet the clinical psychologist. She was and continues to be the most intelligent, soft-spoken woman I have ever met. I still call her occasionally to run something by her. She felt that Andy (besides being absolutely adorable which ingratiated her to me forever) had symptoms of PDD, which hopefully would resolve themselves over time with speech and occupational therapy and a specialized school setting. She spent over six hours with us — both in testing Andy and in educating me. There was so much to do it was difficult to absorb. She also said that if I did nothing else I had to change the approach to speech therapy. Tying him to a chair was not the way to go. I was glad to hear that. This had been my gut instinct all along. I went home and found a new speech therapist the next day. Frankly, I'm not sure how much the years of speech therapy really helped Andy. He didn't learn any of the words they tried to teach him, but he certainly loved to watch the gears move back and forth on the toy boxes. The toys themselves sat idle.

The day before I went back to Boston, my friendly neighborhood developmental center called to tell me they could fit in a full
evaluation for Andy on November 29. I was happy with Boston
but I figured, "Why not? The more, the better." Wrong again! They
put together a group of "specialists" equal in size to the Mormon
Tabernacle Choir. I think their staff plumber may have even been
there. There was little twenty-pound Andy standing in the middle
being poked, measured, stared at, discussed, and the list goes on.
We arrived at nine o'clock in the morning and finally got home at
dinnertime. No two-year-old could have handled a situation like
that, much less a child like Andy.

The developmental pediatrician was the worst of the group.
We had to wait in a room that could only fit two chairs for forty-
five minutes while he ate lunch! The thing I remember most about
his consultation was telling us that his five-month-old baby son
was more aware of his surroundings than Andy was. That sure
made us feel good!

At the end of the day, the troops got us together and told us
that Andy had severe autistic disorder with probable cognitive
impairment. The prognosis was grim. It was as if they killed my
son on the spot and left me with a shell of a child. It took me years
to get over that experience. It was one of the worst days of my life.
They recommended that we join a support group and have a
Fragile X test performed, which I did, and it was negative. Fragile
X syndrome, called Martin-Bell syndrome, is a genetic disorder
and is the most common form of inherited mental retardation.
The support group didn't go as well. I went to a local Center for
Outreach and Services for the Autism Community (COSAC)
meeting the following week. The topic that night was choosing a
lawyer for your retirement years when you could no longer care
for your adult disabled child. I never went to another COSAC

meeting — I decided I'm not the support group type. Besides, Andy was a genius and would be taking care of *me* in my retirement years.

Over the next several months, I began the process of setting up Child Study Team meetings with my local school system. Legally, Andy would be eligible for special services at the age of three. Our town has an excellent preschool handicapped program. In fact many of the families moved here just for that reason. It was a full-day program, five days a week, with only the month of August off.

There were two classrooms with a maximum of eight students each. Each classroom had a lead teacher and three aides. There was also the director, a very knowledgeable, hands-on woman, and staff physical, occupational, and speech therapists. The evaluations were done in my home with a psychologist, a learning consultant, a social worker, and a speech therapist. Andy performed exactly as I expected — he did nothing. He did not acknowledge their presence upon arrival, during the sessions, or on their departure. He did not respond to his name or any directions. In fact he spent the entire time rolling around in a pile of clean laundry. This was one of his favorite pastimes. He must have liked the texture of the clothes. Needless to say, it was immediately agreed that he needed the special services. Down the road, I found out that they were genuinely far more concerned than they let on at the time. They were very professional and probably figured that upsetting me too much would be counterproductive. They were right!

That first year in school was a difficult one. At just three years old, Andy was not used to boundaries. He was forced to sit during circle time, eat lunch with his peers, and generally act like a part of the group. After about four months he realized that he had no choice and calmed down. The highly structured school day seemed to comfort him, as he needed sameness. Transitioning from one activity to the next, however, was always a problem.

The best thing to come out of that first year was Katie, one of his aides. She loved him dearly and would always be there in a crisis (several per day), holding him, cuddling with him, and talking to him. She would give me updates on his progress via the daily notebooks that we sent back and forth. I began having her baby-sit for Andy on the rare occasions she had time. Ron and I would go out to dinner together solely based on Katie's schedule. [It's been eight years now. She has her Ph.D. in psychology, owns a camp for disabled children, and is an invaluable member of our family. None of my children would be where they are today without her guidance and insight, not to mention her ability to both roll with and take the punches!]

Anyway, Andy made it through the first year of school, but there was still no language. Attempts at teaching him sign language failed as well. He was not toilet-trained. He could not hold a pencil, much less draw, color, or paint.

That summer, with fear and trepidation, we decided to spend a week at the beach. As with many children like him, Andy hated the sound of the surf and would sit by the fence covered with a towel or walk back and forth along the fence running his fingers along the slats. He would do this until we left for the day. Toward the end of the week, though, he found a stick and proceeded to write his name in the sand. We were shocked! This was the first real indication that something was going on in his brain. As soon as we got home, we gave him jumbo sidewalk chalk. Ron started to write the alphabet in huge letters in the driveway and Andy completed it. This was a breakthrough. He wrote the alphabet over and over. Our entire driveway was pink, blue, and yellow. Unfortunately, we had to wait for rain before he could start over. It had been a great summer.

His second year of preschool started in much the same as the first. It took months for him to accept the routine again. He had a different teacher this year and Katie was no longer there. His teacher had a "tough love" approach to special education, which made me nervous, but I liked and respected her. He was at least making some progress, albeit slow, in socialization. He would now bring an item to someone if he wanted to play, eat, go home, etc.

On Christmas Eve, my mother called and was so excited I could hardly understand her. She had been listening to Annabel Stehli on the radio promoting her new book, *Dancing in the Rain*. Her daughter had been "cured" of autism following auditory integration training (AIT) as a teenager. *Dancing in the Rain* was a collection of parents' stories describing their experiences with AIT (and other interventions). My mother said Annabel described children who sounded exactly like Andy. Without much enthusiasm, since I had done so much reading and networking, I thought I'd seen it all, I called the local Barnes and Noble and had them order the book (along with Guy Bérard's book, *Hearing Equals Behavior*). I also called information and tracked down the Counseling Center in Westport, Connecticut, and made an appointment to begin AIT in late January. Fortunately we lived close enough that no hotels were necessary. I figured I could always cancel later if I got cold feet. As it happened, AIT was a life-altering experience for Andy.

When *Dancing in the Rain* arrived, I read the whole book in one day, then reread the stories that sounded like Andy — at least half of them. I couldn't believe it! All of a sudden, he didn't seem like such an anomaly anymore. These parents were describing children who now played Nintendo and baseball and rode bicycles. I never dreamed of these kinds of miracles for Andy but I was willing to give anything a try as long as it wouldn't hurt him. I brought the book to school and made the staff read selected stories. They were all cynical about AIT but at least they humored me.

We made the three-hour round trip to Westport twice a day for ten days, early in the morning and late in the afternoon, barely avoiding rush hour each time. We had been there once the week before to meet the practitioner, Danny, and to try to get an audiogram of painful frequencies. Not surprisingly, Andy was completely uncooperative. Danny said, "We'll just hit him with everything we have."

The AIT sessions themselves were nightmarish. Andy yelled, screamed, kicked, and tried to bite. During the first fourteen sessions, we had to hold him down the entire time. There was no way you thought anything good was happening — how could he hear the music over his own screaming? None of the stories in *Dancing in the Rain* prepared us for his behavior for those thirty-minute sessions. During the next four sessions, he fell asleep. We took turns patting his face to keep him awake. The last two sessions were great. Andy actually turned on the AIT equipment, the Audiokinetron, himself and set the dials to the correct frequencies. His genius was finally coming through.

His teacher and I had agreed that I would bring Andy to school after each morning AIT session unless he was clearly going to cause problems. He went in about half the time. He was extraordinarily hyperactive. He would get out of his car seat on the way home and jump around the car like a monkey. I prayed we'd make it home alive. After the fourth session (my mother had gone with me this time), we were driving on the Merritt Parkway when Andy saw a stop sign. He stopped jumping around and said, "Look. Stop." My mother screamed. I nearly drove up a tree. He was four-and-a-half years old, and these were his first words.

After the eighth session, (Katie had gone with me this time) and we had made it home only by the grace of God, we found Andy crouched on the kitchen counter under a cabinet. Rhetorically, I said, "Andy, what are you doing?" "I'm standing here." Katie and I looked at each other in shock. "Did he say what I think he said?" We said this in unison. It was the first time he'd ever answered a question. He had actually started to talk during AIT.

Even his teacher admitted that it "shook something up." The first regular day back to school she wrote:

> We're noticing some positive changes in Andy. He sits in circle for longer periods of time — and participates from time to time. Transitioning is much easier. We are going to start raising our expectations of him — especially during our structured part of the day.

Three days later the notebook reads:

> "Words cannot begin to express the change that we have seen in Andy this week. It's amazing! You can see the level of group participation by the amount of projects he's bringing home. At best, my minimum expectation was for Andy to *sit* at the small group table anticipating his involvement at a future time. Boy, did he surprise us. Lots of language also. All in all, everything seems to be coming together for him.

The director approached me and said that since Andy no longer presented as autistic but as attention deficit disorder (ADD), perhaps we should look into ritalin. She meant this to be a negative comment about his behavior but it sounded wonderful to me — he wasn't "acting" autistic. (I looked into ritalin and decided it was not necessary, but that I would consider it in the future. I never needed to.)

The following month, Scott was born. Andy loved to stare at him in his crib or bouncy seat. I remember one hot day in May while I dried my hair, Andy dressed Scott in the clothes I had laid out on the bed. He had secured seven snaps and put Scott's booties on. Four months earlier, he could barely dress himself, much less a newborn. Gary adored Scott and so did Bryan. He was the ultimate spoiled child.

The next two years were challenging. Andy could clearly read, or at least decode. He started reading billboards, road signs, license plates, anything he could get his eyes on (this is known as hyperlexia). *Wheel of Fortune* was his favorite program — we couldn't miss it. He would constantly check the clock waiting for the magic hour of 7 P.M.

He continued to be very active. I refrained from calling him hyperactive because I felt he needed the time and space to develop and "catch up" to other children his age. One thing that helped was a chiropractor. Someone had mentioned seeing a difference in an attention deficit/hyperactivity disorder (ADHD) child following a visit to a chiropractor, and sure enough, Andy was immediately calmed down after a spinal adjustment. He had been completely out of alignment. The first month or two after the initial appointment, he went three days a week. He still goes once a month.

Andy was toilet trained just before his fifth birthday, by Ron, in two days. He has never had an accident. We also experimented with visual retraining, as he still squinted when staring at a favorite toy. He wore his prism lenses for about a year. I feel that they helped him marginally, but we discontinued them after he threw them at his teacher. Why give him ammunition?

He actually started kindergarten at age five. He was (and still is) classified "autistic." He had his own aide and was pulled from class often for speech and occupational therapy, but he thrived academically. It was during this time that I learned of a study going on at Rutgers University whereby children with central auditory processing disorders were playing computer games. Developed by Dr. Paula Tallal, the concept was one of providing mental calisthenics in order to increase the brain's processing time and ability. I called Rutgers to try and get Andy into the study. To me he sounded like a perfect candidate, especially given the success of AIT. Unfortunately, the study had already closed and Dr. Tallal had moved to California.

By the time Andy turned six, Dr. Tallal's program, known as Fast ForWord, had become available to the public. As luck would have it, my speech therapist and a learning consultant friend of hers were just getting into this business. Andy and one other little boy (age seven) were their first clients. The boys went every day after school from 4 to 6 o'clock starting October 1 and ending mid-December — it took them both about ten weeks to complete the program with acceptable scores. Fast ForWord involved playing a total of eight specifically designed computer games, only three games per day, over and over again while wearing headphones. They were required to follow instructions received via the headphones, which increased in tone and frequency as they neared completion. The Fast ForWord program proved to be very helpful for Andy. He began to answer questions on a regular basis. His processing time improved immediately, and his teacher reported better reading comprehension.

Andy was now in first grade and doing well. When he turned

seven, his teacher and I decided to have him repeat first grade, due in large part to his immaturity and delayed social skills, but also to reinforce what he had been taught (and possibly missed) before and during Fast ForWord. That extra year in first grade made all the difference. He made a few friends and learned how to play Nintendo. He could get to levels no one had seen before. Even his older brother, Gary, was impressed, and his peers worshipped him. Many parents don't like video games. My feeling is that if it makes him "part of the crowd" and helps his self-esteem, it's fine with me!

During this time, there was another obstacle to overcome. He started developing warts all over his hands. They were even in his cuticles and pushing under his fingernails (another symptom of an immune system deficiency, perhaps?) His pencil grasp was still immature, and he had difficulty writing. They must have been painful although he never complained about them. The dermatologist said to leave them alone, that they always go away eventually. It was time for another call to my sister. He had over thirty warts removed surgically. They never returned. He could now hold his pencil normally. We then discovered that he had a gift for drawing. He could exactly replicate any cartoon character without a picture. He had a photographic memory as well. They call these "splinter skills" in autistic children and "talents" in normal children. How unfair!

Andy has just graduated from fifth grade with straight As. He is almost twelve years old and will be starting middle school. His vocabulary and spelling are years ahead of his grade level because he learns the English language by reading the dictionary, not by seeing words in context. He is also a gifted math student. He plays the piano extremely well for someone who never practices; in fact, his piano teacher says he has perfect pitch. He is an enthusiastic Boy Scout and is popular with his peers. He even plays baseball. More importantly, he is kind, polite, sensitive, responsible, and loving. His brothers adore him. When you ask Scott (who is now seven and quite popular) who his best friend is, he says without hesitation, "Andy." When I tell people that he was once profoundly autistic, they quite frankly don't believe me. He is a normal, in fact, exceptional, child with a bright future. He is a true miracle!

BRYAN

Bryan is my "miracle in the making." As a baby, his eyes were bigger and bluer than Andy's and he was chubbier than Andy. In fact, we used to call him "Porky." He started out sleeping in a doll crib by the side of my bed because Andy was still using the regular crib. He was a feisty little baby. He actually turned over at three weeks. He had been crying hysterically and somehow pushed himself over. It was time to get a bigger crib. Obviously, I watched him like a hawk after having missed so many signs in Andy. I wasn't going to have any problems with this child, I thought to myself. He's completely different than Andy had been. He started rolling over, sitting, and crawling on schedule. He walked at thirteen months, he babbled, he waved bye-bye, and he responded to his name. He played appropriately and imitated his brothers, which was bittersweet since Andy's "play" was not what I wanted him to learn.

Bryan had his first ear infection when he was five months old. A single dose of amoxicillin took care of the problem. At seven months, he developed another one. This was the beginning of chronic ear and throat infections. For the next six months, he was on a constant stream of antibiotics. Augmentin was the worst for him — his diaper rash was so bad that it bled for weeks. Dr. Taylor recommended a local ENT, with whom I was finally able to make an appointment after a three-week wait. At my insistence, he agreed to perform a myryngotomy and adenoidectomy, although he would have preferred to wait until Bryan was older. I was not going to have a repeat of the experience I had had with Andy. So, at fourteen months Bryan had tubes in his ears and his infections immediately cleared up.

By the age of sixteen months, Ron became concerned about Bryan's lack of understandable speech. He began reading to him for several hours a day. By doing this, he had taught him about a dozen words, although it wasn't easy. Bryan's interest in books was much less than Gary's had been at the same age. All in all he was progressing well, although his spoken language was slightly less than that of most sixteen month olds. His receptive language appeared normal. I was not overly concerned.

At a regular check-up when he was twenty-two months old, Dr. Taylor noticed that only the left tube remained in place. The right one had fallen out. This information bothered me, as I was concerned about uneven hearing.

By the time Bryan was two, we knew there were problems. The few words Ron had taught him he lost. He began to walk on his toes, which I knew by this time was a classic sign of a neuro-logical problem. Whenever he was excited about something he would flap his hands (to this day, I still call him "the flapper"). He was different than Andy in so many ways, but the similarities could not be ignored. It was time to head back to Boston and start the Child Study Team in motion. By this time, I was an old hand at this stuff!

We were able to see the clinical psychologist in Boston four months later. Again, she did a thorough testing job and felt that Bryan had difficulties in language development, probably related to auditory processing, and somewhat limited social interactions, but not enough to be diagnosed as PDD or autism. She felt that the preschool handicapped program would be perfect for Bryan. At this point, I had already started bringing him to my favorite speech therapist. He was also spending at least one day alone each week at my mother's house (I had stopped working after he was born), where he had her undivided attention. She would set up little games for them to play, which forced him to interact with another human being. You could tell that he loved this time with his grandmother.

The Child Study Team meetings with Bryan went well; in fact, much to my delight, the same four people who had evaluated Andy arrived at our house. This was helpful because they could make reasonable comparisons. They found him to be curious and inquisitive, but extremely shy. His eye contact was limited but did exist. He did not speak at all, but seemed to understand at least some of what was being said. He clearly needed the special program. So, two months after his third birthday, he began the summer session of preschool. Unlike Andy, Bryan was one of their easiest students. He was so shy and nervous around people (almost fearful) that he did whatever he was told and never made a fuss. Unfortunately, it's the easiest children that get the least amount of attention. He had intensive speech and occupational therapy, including "brushing," a technique designed to heighten their senses and put them at ease.

Within a month of starting preschool, I signed Bryan up for AIT in Westport with Danny. Whatever had worked for Andy, I was going to try for Bryan. The initial audiogram was no more informative than Andy's had been. The sessions were easy — Bryan seemed nonplussed by the whole thing. He put the headphones on himself, sat through the session compliantly, took the headphones off, and waved bye-bye to Danny. Each day was the same — there were no instantaneous, dramatic changes. There were, however, gradual changes. He did start to talk more, not conversationally, but meaningful speech nonetheless. He also showed more interest in other children who would be in the house. Besides his brothers, we had a constant stream of visitors. The following February during winter break, I told him it was time to use the toilet. He said, "Okay," and that was the end of that — he was trained.

Bryan ended up going through the preschool program for three years instead of the customary two years. He was very shy and immature. During this time, in addition to school-related services, I sought the help of an occupational therapist in my neighborhood who specialized in sensory integration therapy. Bryan's favorite activity was to go to our swing set, lay his stomach across one of the canvas swings, twirl himself around until the cords were twisted to the top, and let go. Most children wouldn't be able to stand up. Bryan would simply walk away giggling.

He loved going to his OT sessions if for no other reason than the huge tire swing right in the middle of the room. He was rewarded with five minutes on the swing at the end of the session if he did a "good job." He never once did a "bad job." His sensory integration therapy lasted about two years (one session a week for forty-five minutes). It was very successful for Bryan. Among other things, he learned how to better control himself. He seemed more comfortable in his own skin.

Bryan started kindergarten at the age of six with the same teacher Andy had had. He was (and still is) classified "communication impaired." Apparently no neurologist was willing to call him autistic. As long as he gets the services he needs, I don't care what they call him. It was a good yet uneventful year. The summer after kindergarten, Bryan, too, went through the Fast ForWord program. It took him at least eleven weeks to complete all the games with acceptable scores. Again, there were no dramatic changes but certainly there were gradual ones. Bryan learned how to play Nintendo (I no longer had to pay his brothers to play so he could watch) and is now better at it than Andy. When Bryan was seven-and-a-half, I found a neurologist who was willing to give him secretin (a natural pig hormone that became one of the new crazes in the fight against autism). The only problem was that I had to find it myself — once it became a craze, they took it off the market. It took a month, but I tracked down two doses at a pharmacy in Brooklyn. For the sum of $600, they shipped it to me. The secretin was administered intravenously, which was not a pleasant experience, but Bryan responded well. He was less fearful, whiny, and anxious.

Today, at the age of ten, Bryan has just finished the third grade with As in math and science and Bs in everything else. He goes to the chiropractor regularly with Andy. He is an adorable, intelligent, talented little boy with a wonderful sense of humor. He absolutely loves his piano lessons but will not play in front of anyone but his piano teacher. Although he does not like school, I'm hoping and praying for a positive year in fourth grade. He will have an excellent teacher and a wonderful aide who loves him. This is the most important thing to me — that my children are surrounded by people who love them. It is the only effective way for them to learn.

The question as to why two of my boys have been "blessed" with the challenges they have is a mystery to me but a blessing nonetheless. They have taught me what is really important in life. I just finished reading a book entitled *Late-Talking Children*, by Thomas Sowell. I wish I had read the book ten years ago. It would have verified my feeling that, in the face of criticism and adversity, when it came to my children, my gut instincts were always correct. For any parent who has a child like Andy or Bryan, I highly recommend this book. These children really will change the world.

JAMES

―――⚮⚮⚮―――

James Williams

(James received AIT when he was four, for delayed and disordered speech and extreme social aversion. His progress afterward is described in "James" in Dancing in the Rain. *He received AIT again at age six, and once more at thirteen. His writing ability developed along with his speech, and at age eight, he and his mother coauthored* The Self-Help Guide for Special Kids and Their Parents *[Jessica Kingsley, 2000]. At thirteen, he completed his first novel,* Out to Get Jack *[Trafford, 2003]. Since then, he has completed three more novels, and has been a featured speaker at several major autism conferences. James is currently a homeschooled ninth grader. — Ed.)*

CURING AUTISM
Or, Altering One's Perception So It Doesn't Need Curing

Nine years ago a book similar to this one was written. It presents stories of children who made exceptional progress, or were "cured" of their disabilities, by the use of a therapy known as auditory integration training (AIT). The title, *Dancing in the Rain,* described an act that was done by an individual who had benefited from AIT, an act that, owing to the person's autism, was simply not possible before AIT.

In that book, my mother wrote a twenty page essay regarding my life and how I had benefited from AIT. In the following essay, you will read my thoughts not only about treating autism but about "curing" it by not treating it at all.

A BRIEF HISTORY OF MY LIFE

To begin, let me list some of the main events of my life:

- I was told that at the age of two I pushed people out of the front door of my apartment to prevent them from staying, and if they didn't leave, I'd stay in the hall and scream.
- At the age of three, I arranged a tableful of lollipops that were bought from various stores in Manhattan, where we lived. I had to get two lollipops every day — one for each hand — from a number of stores. I spent many minutes examining each one in the store looking for the perfect ones, even though I never ate them.
- At the age of four, I put up road signs in my house, decorating the walls to look like maps and street corners. I became obsessed with alphabet letters and number signs and objects, and soon they would replace the lollipops I simply had to buy when I went into a store. Sometimes my mother would make me work for a special letter or number, such as a solid brass "2," which cost ten dollars. I also had a constant runny nose due to chronic sinusitis.
- At the age of five, I finally learned how to use pronouns, saying "mine" instead of "yours" or "his" or "James's" when referring to myself.

- At the age of six, I entered a Montessori school, unaware of its point and unaware of what I was doing, not knowing why I was there, not knowing why my mother dropped me off and why she picked me up, why there was circle time, just completely ignorant about everything, and trying my best to understand the reasons for school, and why I was always interrupted by everyone despite my determination to work on the Wisdom Cube Puzzle. I was accused of not trying hard enough to tie my shoes, and once my teacher made me walk through deep snow with untied laces to "teach me a lesson."
- At the age of seven, I attended kindergarten for the first time and enjoyed my time with Mrs. Calandra, who accepted me as I was, even though I ignored the other kids and could do more things than they could.
- At the age of eight, I attended second grade, and it was a disaster. I was taken out of school in December, and once out, I helped my mom write a book called *The Self-Help Guide for Special Kids and Their Parents*. I learned more outside of school than in school.
- At the age of nine, I successfully adjusted to a life of not eating wheat-based food after realizing they caused the headaches that plagued me every single day and caused severe carsickness as well for several years.
- At the age of ten, I had a great time attending normal public school again with a teacher named Mrs. Eilhauer, who believed that one should embrace making mistakes rather than fear them, in order to turn them into learning experiences.
- At the age of eleven, when *The Self-Help Guide for Special Kids and Their Parents* was published, I enjoyed normal fifth grade until my classmates began to tease me for the last two

months of the school year. One week after school ended, I developed a mysterious stomach illness that normally strikes autistic children at a younger age.

- At the age of twelve, the stomach problem was ongoing and I could only digest liquid meal replacements.
- At the age of thirteen, I began writing my first book, *Out to Get Jack*, the story of a young autistic boy named Jack Lack and how he deals with the illogical world around him. My intention in writing the novel was to complete something after various years of failed attempts to finish something long and complex. In the real world, I do not make sense sometimes. In *Out to Get Jack*, Jack makes sense.

These events are far from normal, reflecting that I still do not lead a completely normal life and never will. I have problems resulting from my autism, but I also have to deal with social assumptions that I believe are wrong. Although others assume that I am cured of autism, I truly do not believe I am. This is not to say that I have not greatly improved from earlier times. But I did that not by curing my disorder, but by turning it into something that is not regarded as much of a disability.

DEFINITION OF A DISABILITY –
THE WISDOM OF DUMBO

Do the events of my life indicate a hopeless disability? In one sense, yes, for I still cannot do various things that are normal, and I'm terrified of things others wouldn't normally be scared of, but the question is: How many of the things I have trouble doing are necessary actions in order for someone to live a happy life, or at least, an independent life? On the other hand, many of the things that I can do extremely well are regarded as pathological or "splinter" skills, such as memorizing entire road maps or detecting visual subtle differences, as in the lollipops that I chose so carefully when I was three. My mom was frequently advised by doctors and therapists to take away my letters and numbers, discourage my interest in road signs and maps, and force me to play with other kids, despite my terror. I feel, though, that had she done all that, I would never have discovered my talents or become an outside observer, who can write about the events around him rather than participating in them. If she had taken away my "symptoms," I would have lost myself.

Let us think, for example, about the story of Dumbo. Dumbo is an elephant who does not fit in because of his big ears. But wait a minute here! His big ears are not his fault.

So why should he be ostracized because of something that isn't his fault? Well, that's just the way things are, even among animals.

However, when Dumbo realizes that his big ears give him the unique ability to fly, he becomes famous and popular for it. Is the problem of his big ears cured? No. His big ears are unchanged and are still a part of him. However, what was initially regarded as a disability is now perceived as a special ability, admired by everyone.

Similarly, I believe that the best thing that a parent can do for an autistic child is not to "cure" him, but to teach him enough so he can function in society, and then find ways to take his disability and problems and turn them into something useful. For any ability or trait, as useless as it may seem, can someday become of use. I doubt Temple Grandin would have been able to revolutionize animal facilities if it weren't for the "autistic" terror she felt in a world she did not understand and her realization that animals were just as baffled and terrified of the manmade world as she was.

Therefore, when you see your autistic child lining up cards, for example, don't punish him for "perseverating," drug him to stop this "obsessive" behavior, or put him in behavior modification programs to "extinguish" this autistic behavior. Don't see it as "acting strangely." See him as the architect or draftsman he could become, designing the strongest buildings or drawing the straightest lines.

THE EVOLUTION OF AN ABILITY

When you go to an orchestra concert, it seems that the musicians play effortlessly. The violinist makes it seem very easy to play a violin, and someone could get the idea that anyone can play a symphony the moment they pick up a violin. But it takes a lot of work to become a violinist — and a lot of practice.

The musicians didn't always know how to play their instruments. They learned how to do it. And besides — would you expect an orchestra to play you a symphony after everyone had had only one lesson on his or her instrument? No. But would you discourage them from playing since they couldn't play as well as more experienced people? No. The same is true with an autistic person. He may be nonverbal, he may be unable to tie his shoes or pour his juice, but if you find the one thing that he can do, then you should try to promote it in any way. Encourage him to perform his special ability no matter what it is, and someday it will be useful.

And remember that no talent becomes a wonderful ability instantly. Even the musical genius Mozart didn't start writing an opera the moment he sat on the piano — but his ability to play music eventually led him to write operas.

It took me many years to develop my writing ability in order to finish a book. I began by writing nonsense poems at age four, then I wrote short stories, then longer essays, and finally novels, finishing my first novel when I was thirteen. All along the way, my mother was criticized for letting me play with flashcards, watch alphabet videos endlessly, spend hours at the computer, keep away from other kids, and most of all, stay out of school. All of these autistic behaviors, however, helped me develop my ability.

AIT – HOW I'VE BENEFITED, AND HOW IT CAN BENEFIT YOU

After reading all about ability and developing natural talent, how, the reader may ask, does auditory integration training (AIT) fit into the picture? You might have assumed by now that AIT is completely unrelated — after all, what does it have to do with talent? Well, the truth is, my proposal to turn disability into ability does not mean that AIT is useless. AIT is actually an essential part of the process. For in order to get someone to develop and use his talent, other things must come first. And if it weren't for AIT, I would have been unable to begin to develop my ability. Before AIT, I was only able to write nonsense. My typing was my form of babbling. One of my early writings was entitled, "Ostrich Peemint," and went like this: "Anker wacker wichwack cheese fewick." I could decode words on a page but didn't understand them. Since reading and typing came before speaking, they were my "native" language. Speaking was a second language to me. Speaking, however, was essential for me in order for my writing ability to evolve, and I did not pick up speaking until I had AIT. I remember having problems talking, then suddenly I was able to talk after AIT, and I was shocked that I could do so. As a result, AIT was essential as it gave me the ability to turn my curse into a blessing. What I am today is the product of this therapy.

The ideal "cure" for autism is to first give language to one's child, no matter how. The next step is to give him the ability to understand. Then you can encourage him to use his talents and he can communicate the things that he is interested in to you. But you need to start understanding him as well. Don't just modify his behavior or drug him so he doesn't care what happens to him. If he is licking the walls, ask him why. Chances are he needs the oral stimulation to help him talk better. He is not misbehaving; he is trying to heal himself.

I do not remember a lot about my life before AIT. I remember being changed but not what it was like before the change. One of the first changes of AIT was the sudden ability to sit comfortably in a restaurant. Since I have zero memories of actually causing trouble in a restaurant, I cannot make a comparison. I do, however, remember sitting down in a restaurant and not causing trouble. It was the second day of AIT, and my mom said it was the first time I could sit without diving under the table or knocking the silverware on the floor. The same is true of all the therapies I had. I remember being unable to do something, and then, as if by magic, suddenly being able to do it, and not knowing why.

WHAT HURTS THE CAUSE OF HELPING THE AUTISTIC PERSON

What can hinder the development of a person with autism are society's assumptions that the person does not do something because he is unable to and that he must be forced to learn that thing regardless of whether he wants to or not. There is also an assumption that autistic people, who prefer to be alone must be horribly unhappy, and therefore, social events and friends must be forced upon them to make them happy. To me, this is as faulty as the assumption that when a black man walks down the street, an unenlightened person might think he is a drug-dealer, an escaped convict, or a thief.

One assumption that society makes is that everyone enjoys getting presents during the holidays. I, however, hate receiving presents. Every year I ask for nothing and tell everyone that I hate presents, and every year I am showered with gifts that I do not want and do not use. For some reason, everyone understands the desire for presents, but no one understands an aversion to presents. This may sound like a small example, but it leads to all sorts of accusations that I am rude and thoughtless, and that it is my obligation to lie and pretend that I like something when I detest it. Usually the presents that I didn't want in the first place become the subject of a huge battle that I didn't start and yet I am always blamed for it. This does not help me want to interact with other people — quite the opposite.

Also, people automatically make assumptions that because a child has turned five, he can automatically tie his shoes, or comb his hair, or remember to brush his teeth. When an autistic child cannot do these things, he is often seen as bad or obstinate. Then instead of helping him, he is punished, as I was at the Montessori school, or accused of not trying hard enough. It is important to remember that the calendar should not dictate when a child is supposed to master a certain skill. When I was in fourth grade and my mother found me in the school hallway struggling with my shoelaces after the bell had rung, she went out and bought me a pair of Velcro shoes, and that problem disappeared from my life.

In fact, assumptions are the worst things you can make about an autistic child. There should be no assumptions in autism. A seemingly meaningless talent can open up an entire world, or the inability to do something can indicate a lack of interest or a simple misunderstanding, not defiance or misbehavior. Before you decide to change something, seek to understand it.

MY TWO CENTS ABOUT WRITING

When I start to write a book, I remind myself that I have learned things differently from others, and therefore can write about things in a different way that seems new and interesting to others, and in some ways, downright hilarious. Writing is also a way to tell people how I feel without having to deal with making fun of a single person, or to know I'm not going to be made fun of by doing so. For example, if I were to say I was against abortion, you'd know that I was against abortion. But if I were to write a story about a woman named Mrs. Banneker who was against abortion and I made fun of people who supported it, you could say that I might be against abortion, but there is no way you can truly know. A hundred years from now, when I am dead and gone, and somebody reads the story about Mrs. Banneker and her anti-abortion beliefs, he or she may associate her with people they know. But can you accuse the writer of making fun of those people? Of course not. The writer never knew them!

When I write, I try to voice my opinion in humorous ways, but having been teased in school, it is one of my first priorities to make sure that my stories do not personally hurt any one person, but only a group that believes in certain things.

Now that I write a lot, I am no longer frustrated when no one can understand me. When I can't explain myself in person, I just put my thoughts into a book. When I am writing, no one is arguing with me about of my beliefs, and when I want to say something that I believe is true, I put it in a work of fiction. Literature has been an outlet for many ideas in history. Laws may tell us how we should behave and how we should be, but if you want to find out what mankind is really like, look at his creative works.

MY OWN HISTORY OF FAILING TO MEET
SOCIETY'S ASSUMPTIONS

One of the worst accusations made against autistic people is that they don't "fit into" society or that they lack social skills. We are always accused of being ignorant of the rules whereas often we know the rules just fine but simply do not accept them.

My most dramatic experience where I challenged the assumptions of society involved challenging the gender line. There were certain things I expressed an interest in that people could not accept simply because I was a boy. This didn't make sense to me. When I was interested in something, why did it matter whether I was male or female? (Of course, I know now, but back then, I couldn't understand.) Sometimes I wished I were a girl instead.

One day, I attended my sister's preschool spring festival. During the festival, there were tables offering various things that one could do. Right next to the section where one would get his or her face painted was a station where one could get his or her nails polished. I was curious as to what it was like to get one's nails polished, and even though I did not care for the idea, I had not experienced it and knew I did not have to experience it ever again after I had done it once.

I sat down and asked for my nails to be painted red. The person at the table painted them red, and I felt proud that my nails were painted. I showed them to my mother with happiness. But my mother went crazy, along with everyone else I showed the nails to. Little did I realize that I had shocked everyone because I was a boy whose nails were painted, and boys did not wear nail polish. The more people who saw them, the more questions I had to answer. They wondered why a boy wanted to paint his nails. Then other boys around me asked their parents if they could get their nails painted because I was a boy and had my nails painted, but the parents must have said that I was weird and that they weren't going to be allowed to.

Then during the summer, when I was at the beach, an event occurred that involved dignity more than bias. My sister and I, dressed in T-shirts and shorts, were allowed to wade in the water. My sister complained that she was too hot. Because of definitions of nudity that she did not know at the time, my sister could not take off her shirt because it would expose something that could not be uncovered. I could not understand at the time why she couldn't do it. I realized that I wanted to challenge the rule to see what would happen. I also had remembered taking off my shirt in the past and not getting in trouble. So why would my sister get in trouble?

I realized that if she was going to get punished, so would I. So I took off my shirt. What shocked me, however, was that I did not get in trouble, nor was I even noticed. When my sister said to Mom, "But he was able to take off HIS shirt!" my mother said to her, "That's because he's a boy!" I could not understand what was happening, and I did not learn the truth until an hour later.

During a visit to my aunt and uncle's house, I saw a book in one of the bedrooms. Although I had nothing else in common with my cousin Erika, she and I both liked the book, a catalog for a series of dolls and books known as the American Girls Collection. It was a series that was formed to teach girls about history by writing historical fiction involving various heroines. Although I am not a girl, I was interested in the stories. I became obsessed with them while reading the catalog, and you can imagine the trouble that I got into when my mom learned about my obsession. She even said to me, "I had hoped during the visit that you wouldn't find that magazine, because I knew that you'd get obsessed with the American Girls Collection if you did."

I didn't know that what I had done was wrong or that I wasn't supposed to be interested in girl stuff. After reading some of the books, I discovered that girls were often expected to learn how to make something called a "sampler." I was interested in learning how to do this, too, and remembered that my aunt knew how to knit blankets. I wanted to learn how to knit. (Little did I know at the time that samplers were made not by knitting but by embroidering.) I learned that my mom knew how to knit, so I asked her to teach me. I learned it, and became a spectacle yet again. Knitting was very calming to me, but everyone was shocked when they saw me doing it. To them, I was the first boy they had ever seen knitting! Whereas I could not understand their shock! And I also learned that because of that, it was sometimes impolite. Once, I accidentally embarrassed Mom when knitting in the waiting room at a doctor's office. I had no idea that it was impolite.

What am I to do about all of this? Of course, I do not want to change the world, and will not. This is not my plea for changing the rules. I am learning to live with the absurdities of social life. But I do know one thing: Whenever I do not agree with something, it does not matter whether I say so or not as I can always write about it in a book. Again, my autistic talent is helping me to cope with my problems. And besides, the American Girls Collection presented me with historical stories of what I had been personally fighting — the domination and oppression of one group over another (in this case, males over females) for thousands of years. The American Girls stories taught me that, throughout history, no one has liked being told that they're wrong and that they have to do things someone else's way, especially if that way is harmful or makes no sense. These stories led to long discussions with my mother and father about women's rights and how women had no real power until this century, when the feminist movement began. As an autistic person, I could understand the stories, perhaps better than the girls they were written for.

CONCLUSION

Although I have talked on and on about other parts of my life, I must admit that all of my abilities to do things today would not have existed if it weren't for AIT. For I may have the ability to feel something, but what good is it if I can't communicate it to others?

Human beings, after all, know nothing about others except what others communicate to them. But if we see someone doing things and cannot communicate with him, then we have no idea what is going on. It is a mystery to us, for example, as to what it really feels like to have Alzheimer's disease. That is why it is more important to teach an autistic child appropriate language before anything else.

AUTISM'S GREAT DIVERSITY — A DISCLAIMER

When searching for your child's special talent, remember that autism is a diverse disorder. As a result, not all autistic children may even have a special ability. Some kids may have more than one. A therapy that works for one autistic child may fail for another. Every autistic individual is so unique that we can say that the problems of one child are a disorder unto itself owned by that one child, and only that child.

But what does remain universal is this — the only true cure for autism is a cure that turns the individual's talents into functional skills. Buying lollipops may not be a useful talent but observing, evaluating, judging, selecting, sorting, and organizing them provided me with skills I would later need as a writer. Road signs and maps may seem like an autistic interest, but my mother would have gotten lost hundreds of times without me as her navigator.

Learning to function is a long journey, involving many side trips down a long road. I have not completed this journey yet, and still have a ways to go. But I can see that my car is still on the road, and that at least for now, I am not "out of gasoline."

KATIE

——◈◈◈——

Tamra Garner

"I FEEL SOFT NOW"

Something was not quite right. I knew it. But I didn't know where to turn. I remembered reading a story many years before about a girl whose hearing was too intense, whose mother pursued an unorthodox treatment for her that made all the difference. If only I could remember

My second child, Katie, was born on a blustery December day, and her life seemed to stay blustery from that day forward. From the first days of her life, irritability just seemed to permeate Katie's being. She did not want to be held. Her body seemed tense and rejecting. While most newborns squeak, purr, and hum while they sleep, not Katie. If her little throat cooed during sleep, Katie would awaken screaming, unable to be soothed. Day or night, the longest she slept was forty-five minutes.

At nine months, when most babies are making "mama, dada, baba" sounds and starting to have a baby-talk word for a few things, Katie began modeling after my speech. Comprehension may not have been possible, but clearly Katie could hear the specific sounds of my speech at a very early age. After putting her in the stroller to go for a walk one day, she repeated the sounds of the question I had just posed to her, "Reddytogonaw."

As she grew, though, Katie had difficulty picking up on the social messages being conveyed. One evening her exasperated daddy told his overactive preschool daughter to behave. I watched from the next room, while Katie paused and looked at him. She came to me with a puzzled expression. "Mommy, what's a have?" She said it to rhyme with "gave." Since she wanted to please her daddy, she would "be a have" if she could figure out what it was.

Screaming rages began at age three and continued. This was not a child who was expressing frustration with discipline, throwing a tantrum. The rage seemingly came out of nowhere. The only way Katie would calm enough to take a nap was if I lay at her side in absolute silence, modeling slow, deep breathing and stroking her face with a feather-light touch.

Katie attended a small, private school. Her kindergarten teacher began to echo other voices of the past (grandparents, day-care provider, Sunday school teacher, etc.), saying, "Katie is not working up to her potential. She needs to be better disciplined." If only they knew!

My university degree is in Child Development/Family Resource Sciences. I had worked as a child protection caseworker, had trained foster families, and was at the time training parents of high-risk families and the professionals who worked with them, under a federal research grant. And yet, my child lived as though everyday life was pushing her over the edge.

Quite frankly, it was pushing me over the edge. I felt inept as Katie's mother. Her rages were getting to me. I did not want to react to them with anger of my own. I just didn't know what to do.

Katie gave me the first verbal clues that confirmed my suspicions. Upon coming home from kindergarten each day, Katie's one desire was to go to our quiet backyard and swing by herself for up to two hours. Her comments on her way through the house were voiced with a wide-eyed frantic expression, saying, "It was so loud at school today, Mom. It was so loud."

I remembered the story, read so long ago, about the girl whose hearing had been too intense, and wished I could remember more. I began to ask questions, but no one knew the answers.

Katie entered first grade. She came home one day, frustrated at having received demerits. She said the teacher did not understand that she had fallen out of her chair. I asked how that happened, if she had been doing something that would lead her to fall off her chair. Katie matter-of-factly replied, "No, Mom. I was just sitting there and I fell off of my chair."

I about died laughing! My laughter was partly at the situation, and mostly out of relief. It was as if there finally was physical evidence of something not quite right. My daughter had been sitting in a child's chair, and had simply fallen off.

That same month, Katie had a raging outburst at the teacher in the classroom. I visited with Katie's counselor, who suggested a consultation with a specialist. I told the teacher and principal that Katie would be absent for a couple of days while being evaluated for attention deficit/hyperactivity disorder (ADHD). They scoffed at me, both saying, "You need to better discipline this child. There is no such thing as ADHD."

On the five-hour drive to visit the specialist, Katie practiced her reading. She could not remember the three-letter word "and" from one line to the next. She had to be prompted to sound out the word phonetically, as if she had never seen it before. Most of the time, she could not remember the phonetic sounds for the letters.

The specialist's diagnosis was ADHD, Katie was prescribed ritalin, and I was sent to a large bookstore to obtain several books about ADHD. I suggested that Katie pick out a book, too, and she settled on a beautifully illustrated version of Hans Christian Anderson's *The Little Mermaid.* I repeatedly tried steering her to a younger, simpler version of the story, not wanting her to be over-whelmed with the verbiage of the book she had chosen. Not to be dissuaded, Katie left the bookstore with the book she wanted. I left with apprehension.

On the way home, on her first day on ritalin, Katie sounded out the word "grandmother." On her fourth day back in the class-room, Katie's teacher and principal jointly approached me. They asked what I was doing differently, and commented on Katie's much improved behavior and concentration. I then told them of Katie's diagnosis and medication. Stunned, they hesitatingly ad-mitted there must be such a thing as a few real cases of ADHD. Later, they referred another little boy (whom Katie had personally diagnosed with ADHD) to the specialist.

I thought the answer had been found. But there was more to it than a little white pill.

While many of her behavior issues were modified by medica-tion, Katie was still overwhelmed by certain sounds. One day, she plopped down among the many soft pillows on the sofa in our liv-ing room. The stereo was playing quietly in the background at the other end of the room. The door was open to the gentle summer sounds of our reserved little neighborhood. All at once, Katie began yelling, almost screaming, "Stop it! Stop it! Make it stop!"

When I asked her what she was talking about, she wildly ges-tured to the far end of the living room, moaning, "That!! That thing!" Eventually, I got her to tell me, "That ball!" Her brother had dropped a basketball on the carpeted floor sixteen feet from where Katie was sitting. Only when I held it to my ear could I hear the slight hissing sound of air leaking from the ball. Katie was frantically yelling at me, "Make it go away!" while describing the sound as if a tornado were coming through the room. I put the ball outside. She gradually calmed down. My suspicions that her hearing was hyperacute were being confirmed.

But life changed. We moved overseas. Katie and her brother entered an international private school. She flunked out. Her brother passed. I homeschooled them. Katie flunked out. Her brother thrived. Her dad and a private tutor homeschooled the children while I attended classes. Katie with Dad and tutor combined did a bit better, but only while working one on one in an environment that was entirely contained.

We returned to the States. The children entered public school. Evaluations were begun on Katie. Her fifth grade IQ was widely variant, depending on testing conditions (in the corner of a classroom vs. one-on-one in a private hospital room). Everything else was vague. Things weren't entirely normal, but not entirely abnormal either. No diagnosis.

We adopted a child from an Eastern European orphanage. We went to a conference on the developmental challenges often experienced in a child adopted from an orphanage environment. The entire time one researcher was speaking, I kept whispering, "That's Katie! That's Katie!" I spoke to the researcher, who agreed to test Katie. I felt as if there may be hope. I had gotten over blaming myself.

Katie was diagnosed with central auditory processing disorder. She was fitted with ear-molds that have a sound filter embedded in them to help filter out background sounds. This helped to some degree, but many classroom accommodations still had to be made. I developed close working relationships with her teachers, and a fully licensed teacher was employed as a personal tutor on a daily basis. Katie made some improvement at school and made a few friends, whom Katie described as part of the "lowest of the low" social group. When Katie did not wear her ear-molds, the changes in her behavior were painfully evident to everyone.

In the meantime, I had been doing Internet research, and finally had found that story of old. The mother and daughter were Annabel and Georgie. They had brought the unorthodox treatment to the United States.

I fought with our insurance company for over a year to approve auditory integration training (AIT) for Katie. Last summer, we traveled to the next state for Katie to receive AIT. Katie, by then fifteen, was skeptical. After the first visit, she emerged from the treatment room, eyes glazed, attention dazed. Good indicators.

After the sixth day of treatment, we were driving in eight lanes of metropolitan traffic, with engine and traffic sounds everywhere, a siren wailing in the not-so-far distance, the stereo playing inside our vehicle, and Katie's two brothers noisily playing in the back seat. Katie turned to me with a perplexed look on her face, and asked, "I don't get it. Why is everything so quiet?" I laughed with delight.

During our long drive home after Katie's last day of treatment, I asked her what, if any, changes she sensed. She did not respond. I gently prodded. She said she didn't feel like talking in front of her brothers. I asked why. She was afraid they would laugh. Finally, she couldn't contain herself any longer.

"I feel soft, now. I don't feel like I have to be hard and tough all the time anymore. I feel like I could be a 'girly-girl' now. I feel like I could be what I always wanted to be, but never could be before." I was driving down the highway, bawling like a baby, and finally glad that I had been a she-bear, willing to fight for her cub when no one else had a label or a treatment. We have our own story to tell now.

———∞∞———

Katie started her sophomore year the day after her AIT ended. She felt like going cold turkey without a tutor, but I felt she needed to wean gradually. We compromised by utilizing a volunteer college student two days a week only for geometry and biology. About four months into the school year, she further weaned to utilizing a peer tutor for geometry only. Her last grade report was all As and Bs for the first time in her life. She is now handling all of her classes, studies independently, and is doing well.

Katie has blossomed into a confident young woman, who deliriously experienced her first date last fall, and since decided she would rather just be friends with boys for now. She decided independently to limit her contacts with individuals who are making questionable choices, and is nourishing friendships that are supportive and growth-oriented.

Her behavior at home is changing as well. Old, ingrained habits of reacting to frustrating situations with rage are being replaced with healthy communication patterns. The child who used to jerk away from any touch now comes to me most mornings for a long, deep hug. It is like she is trying to drink in all the missed hugs of her previous years.

She is soft now.

SETH

⊶⊷

Teresa Murrow

My son, Seth, started part-time day care when he was nineteen months old. Everything was fine, so we progressed to full-time four days a week.

One day when I went to pick him up, I noticed a bulletin board in Seth's room listing all the children and the words each one was starting to use. Each child had about five to ten words except Seth, who had none. I just hadn't realized anything was different and asked his teacher about it. She said not to worry; a child will talk when he is ready to talk.

We took him to the pediatrician for his two-year physical. She said he was in perfect health. He was not talking because he was just lazy — take him to a speech therapist. Needless to say, the "lazy" part was not what I wanted to hear. I decided to let Seth be the guide of when he would talk.

At day care he was becoming withdrawn and angry. The teachers told us he would often hide under things. He would not participate in group activities. At home with us or his grandparents, he seemed okay and was our beautiful little boy. But we did begin to notice he was becoming overwhelmed by crowds or new places. In a crowd he would not show any eye contact, would move from one thing to another, and become angry when we would try to correct or control him. It was as if he would shut out the world and only focus and see what was in front of him. His speech still showed no signs of development nor did he show any interest in it.

We had someone from Family Services come out to see him. They did an evaluation and told us he was speech delayed and also had sensory integration dysfunction. They told us we needed to take Seth to a speech therapist and to an occupational therapist to help him with his problems. It was explained to us that children with sensory integration dysfunction often have speech delays and with occupational therapy can overcome the sensory problems and then the speech will follow. Thus began our journey to help our son.

Seth had just turned two and said approximately five words. He could not go to many public places because they seemed to overwhelm him. He also had difficulty interacting with more than one or two children. He seemed to be a very angry, unhappy little boy.

Seth was still in day care. They were refusing to move him into rooms with children his own age because of the speech delays, and they felt he was not ready emotionally. I think this only made things worse because he was a two-year-old in a room full of one-year-old children, still doing and learning one-year-old things — which he already knew and did. He was also losing the few friends he had because they were being moved to the other room with children their age. This was isolating him even more.

Family Services told me they were going to help Seth at

school by doing on-site visits to the school once or twice a week. I thought this was going to be a good thing. Something to help Seth through his day and show the school because the fact that he did not communicate like the other children did not mean he did not understand anything. Instead, their help consisted of observing Seth and leaving me a note outlining the things he did wrong that day. Never any suggestions on how to help him.

It was obvious to us that day care was not in Seth's best interest. The decision was made for me to quit working and devote my energies to Seth. We were fortunate that the first speech therapist opened Seth's world to communication through sign language. She proved to be extremely helpful with her guidance and suggestions.

We went through several occupational therapists before our speech therapist recommended one that matched Seth's personality. Seth immediately started responding and showing signs of improvement. He did not seem as angry. He was using sign language to communicate. If he became overwhelmed with things, we learned through occupational therapy how to let him jump and bang his body in a safe, playful way to help calm him down. But along with these improvements, other things, such as loud noises, began to bother him. At first he would just overreact to a loud noise, then eventually he would hide when he heard anything loud (airplane, lawn mower, music, automobile, construction equipment). He had reached a plateau with his sign language. His speech therapist felt he was almost ready for auditory integration training (AIT). She suggested that we take some time off to break the normal speech therapy routine so that he would be more open to the differences in the auditory integration training routine. We decided to increase his visits with the occupational therapist to twice a week.

When Seth was 3, we started the two weeks of auditory integration training. At the time he could say about ten words, had a
short attention span, made little eye contact, was a very picky eater,
and had little interaction with people except immediate family.
Transitions were difficult, crowded places or anything new was too
much, loud noises upset him, and he did not like to play with more
than one or two children at a time.

The beginning of auditory integration training started with
an explanation of the procedure and possible reactions during the
training. Seth did not want to wear the headphones, which made
the first few sessions pretty difficult. We played distraction games
and he eventually accepted wearing them and would only protest a
little and not so loudly. There were only a few reactions during the
training. Mostly his equilibrium was off and I had to watch him
closely because he would lose his balance.

Almost immediately after the sessions ended, Seth just
seemed calmer, as if there was a peacefulness in him I had never
seen. His sleeping patterns improved. Then I noticed some of the
sensory things that had gone away, or gotten better, were starting
to come back such as the crowds bothering him, the banging game
returned, and the anger came back. I also noticed that when he
would try to draw or do something with his right hand, his left
hand would curl up in an awkward fist in the air. This lasted about
a month and I kept reminding myself what my speech therapist
had explained to me. That the sensory issues could return briefly
but they would slowly disappear as his auditory system became
stronger.

Then wonderful things began to happen. His world started
to expand. A game or toy previously played with in only one manner now increased to multiple ways. Words started coming — even
five in one night! We could tell that Seth liked being able to com-

municate and he wanted to talk. He was still seeing his occupational therapist, but she felt that he no longer showed any sensory
problems and released him from her care.

In six months, Seth went from five or ten words to multiple
sentences that expressed his thoughts and emotions. He continues
to eagerly repeat new words and try new sentences. Just this alone
has changed our family dynamics. We now know what he wants for
breakfast, what toy he wants to play with, or when he wants to go
fishing with his grandfather. One of the most pleasurable times for
us is at dinner when we each talk about our favorite part of that
day. He often surprises me with what his favorite part of the day
was. He knows and sings his ABCs and likes to point out words
and letters as we drive down the street. He can count to twenty in
English and to ten in Spanish and is learning other Spanish words.
Before this time, I could tell he knew letters, colors, and shapes,
but he wasn't able to tell me or ask about them.

Loud noises no longer bother him. Recently we were outside
playing and a plane flew over. Before AIT, whenever I heard a
plane, I would always become tense, trying to think how I could
help Seth stay calm and not be afraid. But as the plane flew over,
Seth DID NOTHING. It was as if a plane had never even flown
over us. I wanted to sit down and cry, but I knew I needed to just
act as if nothing new had happened and continue to play with
him. Now Seth likes to point to planes and say, "Look Mommy,
plane." Another small, giant step.

Seth has become a happy, outgoing little boy. He talks to
everyone in stores, even giving grocery advice to lost-looking
fathers. When we go to the playground in the park, Seth doesn't
hesitate to start playing with the other children. I joined a moms'
club because Seth kept asking to play with more kids. Besides
playing with children and his social skills growing, I'm watching

him go to new places, do new things, make sudden changes in plans, and he loves it all.

People who knew Seth before auditory integration training and see him now cannot believe that he is the same little boy. It has been over two years of emotional ups and downs, frustration, anger, heartbreak, etc., and a lot of hard work. But the changes in Seth have made everything worth the effort. This fall will bring another new and exciting step — preschool — but I am confident Seth will handle every challenge.

YONATANI

---◅◈◈◈▻---

An Interview with Psychologist,
Dr. Michal Beeri

ANNABEL: I'd like you to start by giving me a time line of your son's development.

MICHAL: Yonatani was crawling at six months, standing at nine months, and walking at twelve months. He said his first words around fourteen to sixteen months. At twenty months, he was able to say at least eighty words, not very clearly, but understandably. Then at twenty-two months, he developed a huge swollen lymph gland on the left side of his neck. He had to go through endless medical examinations, including a biopsy and a twenty-four-hour hospitalization. Our feeling is that he didn't regress but that his development slowed down significantly.

At twenty-nine months, we moved to the United States from Israel. This transition seemed to have been a very traumatic one for

Yonatani. My husband, who is also very involved with everything concerning the children, moved here on August 1, 2002, but we didn't have my visa until September 12, 2002. My son had only one week of daddy in that period when his father visited. Yonatani was upset by this. He sat all day in front of the TV. I was with him all the time. I had stopped working and he wanted to go to the playground, but all he wanted to do was swing. He had had a nanny since he was three or four months until the day we came here when he was two and a half, but the nanny didn't come with us. He had to go to school for the first time, half a day, and the whole move was very traumatic. For my daughter, it went so smoothly, she learned the language very quickly, she has no social problems so she very quickly made friends and wasn't lonely on the weekends. She would ask when we were going back to Israel, but it was okay. Yonatani's speech, on the other hand, practically stopped developing, and he seemed very confused by English. He started private speech therapy at thirty-six months, which didn't seem to change anything.

ANNABEL: Was there anything besides his delayed speech that sounded the alarm for you at any age before that?

MICHAL: When he was eight months old, he was with my mother-in-law and she said, "Shouldn't he be saying ga ga ga, da da da," and my husband became concerned even then. I didn't think there was anything. Yonatani was very sweet and warm. However, after the move, he seemed very depressed. When he was three, his SLP (speech and language pathologist) asked us to read a book on sensory integration, and that was when I thought I'd found my child. The SLP was absolutely convinced that he was autistic, from the first moment. But she was still doing her training under supervision, and when she wrote the final report, there was another signature on it, and I had the feeling that she wasn't trustworthy, that she was trying to prove she was right at my son's expense. Her cousin was an occupational therapist and she said Yonatani had SSI (sensory integration issues), eye contact problems, etc. Whether it was autism or not, she didn't know. Then I decided, "I don't care what she says." I don't know what originally caused my son's issues. There is a genetic problem. My daughter, for instance, didn't touch the grass until she was four. She will say something is smelling and I'll take her where it is and it will be a diaper or something — downstairs. She is hypersensitive to smell. There is something in the family going on.

ANNABEL: Yes, there is a genetic factor, I'm sure, but it wouldn't account for the degree of dysfunction your son has experienced; it's just there as a given. The antibiotics and all the manhandling that went on, and how helpless he felt when he experienced the separation when he had to go the hospital — this might have exacerbated his basic condition but it wouldn't have caused it.

I also think you can pretty well discount the emotional factors as a cause for developmental problems. Children know they are loved. They know when they're loved and they know when they aren't and the damage is done whether the mother is there all the time or not, and you obviously loved him from the minute he was born. This sounds like a sensory processing thing to me. You can't control your hearing, and that can be maddening when you have hyperacute hearing. Fortunately, now he doesn't have to control it anymore, and I'm sure it's going to make an enormous difference. We are talking about sensory processing and someone who reacts differently to sound and touch than other people, and he's confused by this. It's very confusing. We all think our senses are alike and they're not. And also he may have noises in his head that he never thought to try to communicate about. He may think everyone hears them. He may have uncomfortable loudness levels for sounds coming in from the outside, distortion of some sounds not coming in loudly enough, and a form of tinnitus that is beyond anything you can test for. A year from now you are going to be amazed at your child's growth when you think of the progress he has already made in only three and a half months following AIT. And I know you will reinforce the positive gains he makes, and see to it that his progress is validated, respected, and enjoyed. Even nine months from now he may be completely fluent in his speech and you may be wondering what to do with your gifted child.

MICHAL: We have already seen a huge difference in many areas: speech, behavior, and social skills.

ANNABEL: Does Yonatani engage in any creative play?

MICHAL: He imagines a lot now. He understands that it's his imagination. He wants to be the waiter and will take his blankie and pretend it's pizza.

ANNABEL: Imaginative play was something he was good at before AIT?

MICHAL: Yes, but now it's much more complex.

ANNABEL: He may have a lot of creative ability somewhere, and he may have huge assets associated with this sensitive reaction to life. How is his interaction? Does he play with his sister?

MICHAL: He squeezes his sister thinking this is what she likes because he likes it. We put him on the floor with a bunch of pillows on him and then lie down on the pillows and he loves that.

ANNABEL: Temple Grandin's squeeze machine operates on the same principle: deep pressure. And of course, hugs are the greatest therapy if he can tolerate them. Georgie says that if "holding therapy" had been done on her, forcing hugs on her, she would have gone out of her mind because she was too hypertactile, but for some kids it seems to help, and fits right in to treating sensory integration problems. But I think it's better not to force the child. Can he interact with kids his own age?

MICHAL: He can play on physical and playground equipment. But I don't see him yet letting another kid play with him. He'll play with his school bus and who sits in the back and who sits in the front, and then after AIT he took a Tigger doll and turned it to me and Tigger talked to me. That was a big change. When dolls interact now, it's very appropriate.

ANNABEL: That's wonderful. Georgie didn't do this until she was seven. And now that your son's sound sensitivity is resolving, this should improve. After all, your hearing is the only sense you truly can't control and have no sense of being able to control. If you have olfactory issues, if your sense of smell is too acute, you can shut off your nose, making yourself sound as if you have a cold. You can avoid foods that you can't stand. You can avoid touch and you can shut your eyes but you can't walk around with your hands over your ears, or anticipate noises that will bother you and have your hands over your ears in time to keep yourself comfortable.

MICHAL: Speaking of foods he can't stand, I can count on one hand what he eats. Sandwiches with cream cheese or chocolate, no more than that. Pasta but only with honey on it. Has to be sweet. Macaroni and cheese, but it has to be a special kind; once I got the wrong kind and he wouldn't touch it. Grapes. He likes very few things. He is extremely picky and still is. He is far from getting better.

ANNABEL: Have you heard about the gluten/casein-free diet, and the intestinal issues of some of these children, and how toxins are getting into their brains? And that this has to do with the etiology of autism? You're telling me that what he likes to eat is pretty much not what he should eat. Dr. William Shaw is a toxicologist with his own lab that offers a number of tests, including allergy tests. Joan Matthews, who contributed to *Dancing in the Rain*, says that when her son, James, was diagnosed at age eleven with these nutritional challenges, it was the last puzzle piece. Sidney Baker, M.D., is another pioneer in the field. You might want to explore this. If you read *Dancing in the Rain*, the nutritional factors come up all the time. The macaroni and cheese is a real giveaway. James would basically eat only Noodle Roni when he was four. White flour, honey, and sugar are other culprits. One of the factors that might reinforce your son's growth spurt is changes in the diet, and his hyperacute taste buds won't be so hyperacute because of neural pathway spillover after AIT. His sense of taste will modify along with his hearing.

MICHAL: Actually he's more interested in other foods now. He's asking what we are eating, and I get the feeling he may be able to try some new foods.

ANNABEL: Addictive foods are interesting; they are foods that you eat more of than you want. You tend to stop when you're eating lobster or broccoli. It's the foods that turn into sugar quickly that sedate us and make us want to continue eating them because of the effect.

MICHAL: He didn't like the feeling of eating an Oreo when it was put in ice cream. He only likes them by themselves.

ANNABEL: A lot of that will modify as time goes on. I'm sure you'll want to do AIT again.

MICHAL: With AIT, I was extremely concerned at first, thinking he wasn't going to stand it for a minute.

ANNABEL: But it feels so good.

MICHAL: Then he sat for the whole half hour, perfectly, and then for an hour after the AIT he would blurt out gibberish.

ANNABEL: An explosion of jargoning. I'm sure he did that because his own sounds didn't impact on him in an uncomfortable way.

MICHAL: Two weeks after the AIT, we started noticing a change in Yonatani's speech capabilities and also in his attention. He had it last December, when he was forty-four months, and in January, he started a full-day program, with a heavy emphasis on speech. We feel there is already a huge difference.

ANNABEL: What about sleeping?

MICHAL: He is sleeping longer since AIT. He goes to bed at eight and we have to wake him at seven-thirty.

ANNABEL: Better sleeping after AIT is practically guaranteed. Is he toilet trained yet?

MICHAL: He is toilet training himself. Actually because I said I'm not starting it until the school helps me.

ANNABEL: Is he in day care or nursery school?

MICHAL: He's in a special program. He was in regular school, hitting other kids and talking during circle time and being different, but they coped with him well. There were two kids there who adored him. Children are smart and they don't want to play with you if you're hitting them all the time, and here were these two kids who adored him. Something in the way he interacts is not that terrible but basically he couldn't stand anybody near him and he used to hit a lot. Now he is in regular school till twelve and then he goes to a special program. Most of the children are like him, without specific diagnoses, autistic spectrum but reasonably functioning in some areas, but a lot of speech problems. In the town where we live there is a full-time school. I didn't want my kid to be with autistic kids because I'm holding out for his not being autistic.

ANNABEL: What is going to happen next year in September?

MICHAL: I'm leaving him in the full-day program until kindergarten or first grade.

ANNABEL: Do you think he'll mainstream into first grade?

MICHAL: Yes, I think so.

ANNABEL: And your husband is absolutely positive that he will.

MICHAL: Yes, he is. What Yonatani was able to say six months ago and what he's able to say now is amazing — such a change after the AIT. He is still far away from being a normally developing four-year-old, but we do feel that he is on the right track, and we know he'll get there.

NICHOLAS

───❈───

Martha Damiani

My husband, Donald, and I longed to start a family soon after our wedding in the summer of 1986. However, we would endure over nine years of infertility before our prayers for a child were fulfilled. Conceived naturally (by the grace of God!), and after a textbook pregnancy, our first son entered our world on December 26, 1995, via an uncomplicated birth. He was healthy and "perfect"! We named him Nicholas, after Donald's uncle, who had recently overcome a life-threatening form of cancer, and went on to survive many years past doctors' predictions. Little did we understand at the time that our Nicholas would also one day be an "overcomer," and flourish beyond doctors' expectations.

During the first year of Nicholas's life, he met all the usual developmental milestones. He rarely became sick, and aside from his inability to sleep whenever there was even the slightest noise in the house, and his disdain for being held or cuddled, we felt that Nicholas was a "typical" baby. Donald and I relished our new role as parents and life was sailing along merrily. Shortly after Nicholas's first birthday, we learned to our delight and amazement, that we were expecting our second child.

In the months that followed, when Nicholas's pediatrician mentioned a possible language delay, we dismissed it. He had some words, and lots of babbling gibberish, and we had read that boys can take longer to develop language. He was a playful and seemingly happy toddler. When Nicholas was nineteen and a half months old, our second "miracle" child was born. Anthony arrived two months after my fortieth birthday, but six and half weeks early! He was healthy and holding his own, despite his early arrival. Donald brought Nicholas to the hospital to see his new brother for the first time, and I recalled that he looked a bit disinterested, but I was glad that he at least wasn't jealous! Sitting in that hospital room, with my husband and our two long-awaited sons, I had felt that life was simply perfect. But things were soon to change, and dramatically.

⸺ ∞ ⸺

Because of Anthony's prematurity, he had numerous developmental delays. His suckle reflex was lacking, which made it very difficult for me to feed him. He was eventually diagnosed as having aspiration, a condition where the epiglottis does not close properly over the trachea to prevent liquids and food from travelling down the windpipe into the lungs. This condition made it even more challenging to feed him safely. He was eventually evaluated by the state's early intervention program. It was initially speculated that Anthony had cerebral palsy. We were beside ourselves with grief. But we resolved to give him the best chance at a normal life that we could. Anthony qualified for occupational, physical, speech, and developmental therapies, due to his significant delays in fine and gross motor skills, and his feeding issues. For the next year and a half of his life, four therapists came to our house each week to give our son his therapies. Despite this overwhelming intrusion and inconvenience in our lives, this early (and intense!) intervention literally saved Anthony's life. By the time he was thirteen months old, Anthony no longer choked and aspirated on his food or drinks. He had learned to sit up on his own strength, could crawl, and was learning to walk. He finally was able to walk unassisted at fifteen months.

While our focus was so intensely centered on Anthony during those eighteen months, our first son was, unbeknownst to us, quietly slipping away. During therapy visits at our home, my attention was needed for Anthony, and I was so happy that Nicholas was quite content to play by himself in another part of the room or house. Being between two and three years old now, Nicholas was beginning to show some skills that were beyond his developmental age. He knew the entire alphabet, upper- and lowercase, verbally and by sight. He knew all the numbers to 100. He could correctly identify many geometric shapes, such as trapezoids and parallelograms. He could easily assemble twenty-five piece jigsaw puzzles, with no help. He began drawing intricate shapes and designs. He had memorized and could recite flawlessly over twenty-five nursery rhymes. Because of all these skills and interests, Nicholas had many activities with which he could busily amuse himself, while I attended to more pressing matters. I was grateful to have such a "good" child, and relieved that the "terrible twos" was perhaps a myth! Moreover, we were beginning to believe that Nicholas was possibly gifted, since he seemed so "smart" in so many areas.

As the year 1998 was drawing to a close, and as Nicholas turned three, we were beginning to think that our turbulent days of addressing Anthony's many developmental issues were soon ending. Anthony was sixteen months old, and was nearly fully caught up from all his delays. He was a happy and expressive toddler showing no signs of cerebral palsy. Donald and I rang in the new year with a most grateful sigh of relief, and with renewed hope for the future, now that our baby was finally doing well.

――― ∞∞∞ ―――

Two weeks after Nicholas's third birthday, the tantrums suddenly began. He would hurl himself to the floor screaming, flailing his arms every which way, for what seemed to be no reason at all. Sometimes these "rages" would last for forty-five minutes, and they would occur several times a day, every day. "Where had our lovely and bright child gone?" we asked ourselves in bewilderment. We started reasoning that perhaps he was finally going through the terrible twos a little late, since he had obviously missed this developmental milestone. When we had asked his pediatrician about Nicholas's new and odd behavior, she assured us that some children do indeed go through a contentious period a little later in life than most children do at the more typical age of two.

After several more months of tantrum-filled behavior passed, Nicholas began attacking his younger brother. Up to this point, Anthony was not a big factor in Nicholas's life, since Anthony was often preoccupied with therapists, and because he was not yet old enough to be a playmate for Nicholas. But now that Anthony was on the home stretch of his recovery and almost two years old, he was interested in being with his big brother and wanted to do everything he was doing. Unfortunately, it seemed like everything Anthony did irritated Nicholas. If Anthony touched a toy, or tried to hug him, or even spoke to him, Nicholas would push, hit, or kick him. It was utterly painful to watch Nicholas rebuff Anthony's innocent attempts at interaction. And unfortunately, sometimes Anthony would get physically injured by Nicholas's angry outbursts. One time, Nicholas violently hurled a book at him, with one corner of it landing squarely on Anthony's forehead. That bruise took over three weeks to disappear. There were many other times when I'd find Nicholas bashing his brother's head with a toy wooden train. I couldn't even go to the bathroom without taking Anthony with me and locking the door.

Soon, Nicholas began hitting his father as well. When Donald got down on one knee in front of Nicholas to say "good morning" to him one day, Nicholas returned the greeting with a solid punch to Donald's face, knocking him backward. If Donald tried to engage Nicholas in roughhousing, he would pummel his daddy and scream hysterically "NO!!" Donald was finding that there was little he could do with his son that did not cause him distress.

Our attempts to discipline Nicholas in this area of aggressive behavior proved fruitless. No amount of reprimands, warnings, or spankings seemed to have any effect on his behavior. Whenever we'd ask him why he hit Anthony, he'd either repeat the question or he simply did not answer it. Whenever he did reply, his responses were often illogical. Once, we asked him if he would like milk or juice to drink. He replied matter-of-factly, "I'm building a wristwatch." We were beginning to notice that Nicholas would often speak mostly in echoes, or use a phrase he had heard from a TV show, or what he may have heard us say. Rarely did he speak an original idea, and rarely was he able to adequately answer any open-ended question. More often than not, a screamed "NO!!" was what we heard.

Other strange behaviors also began suddenly cropping up. Nicholas became even more clumsy and accident-prone than he had been in his toddler years. He'd run into doorways, bump into furniture, and even trip over his feet, losing his balance frequently.

He was always sporting bruises, and his lower legs in particular, were nearly completely purple at all times. Nicholas could also no longer stand the sensation of clothing on his skin, and would often run around the house naked, save his underwear. He would not feed himself, because touching food, such as sandwiches, made him squeal in distress. He also frequently gagged on his food, as if his swallow reflex was impaired. And most especially, ordinary sounds, like a dog barking, or a chair being pushed under the table, made him so crazed, that he would run out of the room in terror, covering his ears tightly. Eventually, even some of Nicholas's most favorite videos, such as *Thomas the Tank Engine*, were too terrifying for him to watch without his ears covered. Just my picking up one of those tapes to place inside the VCR would make him run out of the room in a panic. He was literally trembling with fear, and yet, he still wanted to watch this show. I just didn't understand why these certain videos were so troubling to him. And of course, he couldn't tell me.

Going shopping as a family had become an ordeal, because all the sights, smells, and especially sounds, would cause Nicholas to have a "meltdown." In vain I tried to assuage his screams while he pelted me, and as I took notice of other people's glares. To be sure, they were silently questioning my parenting skills. As was I at the time. I eventually resolved not to take the boys out shopping again. Or to restaurants, or to church, or to anyone else's house. No matter where we would go, there was no safety.

Other little children were also of particular distress to him. Whenever I would take the boys to the local playground, Nicholas would run away in terror from the other children. He loved to swing, since we had one in our backyard. But at the playground, he would just hide behind me and cover his ears, while his brother played happily. I also remember a holiday occasion when my brother and his wife and four children came over for a visit. As soon as the front door opened, Nicholas ran and hid under our dining room table, to escape from even his very own cousins.

Eventually, the self-injury began. Whenever he became frustrated over his Legos, or a puzzle piece that wasn't fitting just right, he would smack himself on the side of the forehead mercilessly, often with a closed fist. He would also hit himself whenever I verbally reprimanded him. Or when it was time for a bath, or some other activity that was different from whatever it was he was doing at the moment. Any change in routine or activity, any frustration, or any disciplinary action we carried out, would provoke Nicholas to self-injury. It was more than I could bear to watch him do this to himself. In the short space of just six months after his third birthday, when he was yet a darling, docile, and smart young boy, he had disintegrated into an aggressive, oppositional, self-abusive tyrant. It was clear that something was horribly wrong with our first son, but we didn't know what it was.

One early summer day, when the speech therapist was at our home for her weekly session with Anthony, she took me aside to talk about Nicholas. She shared with me all her observations about Nicholas that she had been making to herself during the past year, and I nodded knowingly to almost everything she said. Then she handed me some articles to read. They were all about autism and Asperger's syndrome, a form of autism. She very gently and discreetly said, "I think this is what Nicholas is suffering from." I did not respond to her. I sat there frozen, just staring down at the titles of the articles she had handed me. Before she left, I thanked her for sharing these articles with me, and promised I would read them over. It would be a year later before I fully realized what courage it took for this speech therapist to share her concerns with me. And for her courage and honesty, I am eternally grateful.

As I was began reading those articles, I fought the idea of Nicholas having autism with every fiber in my being. After all, I had a degree in psychology. I had learned about autism, and I was taught that it was a serious but rare childhood disorder. And that it left children in a world of their own, unable to communicate appropriately (or at all), unable to feel human emotion, and that most were also mentally retarded. I was also taught that it was incurable. This could NOT be my son! My head spun as I looked back in time over Nicholas's short life, replaying in my mind all his odd but seemingly (at the time) unrelated behaviors. I read and re-read the diagnostic criteria for autism in the *Diagnostic and Statistical Manual for Mental Disorders*, 4th edition (American Psychiatric Association, 2000), perhaps a dozen or more times. In the days to follow, I could no longer run from what I was slowly starting to realize: that perhaps it was indeed true, that our first son was autistic.

After I spent a full week of crying and mourning the loss of my "perfect" child, I pulled myself together and started reading everything I could get my hands on about autism. Everything we had learned from our experiences with Anthony taught us that early and intense interventions gave a child the best chance at recovery. Donald and I resolved to apply to Nicholas the same kind of energy that we had directed into Anthony's issues. We made an appointment with an autism specialist at the Children's Hospital in Indianapolis. We were told that it would be a six-month wait! During this period of waiting, we had Nicholas evaluated by our local school district. Although his vocabulary and his pre-academic scores were average to good, his scores for expressive communication, socialization, motor skills, and daily living skills were all below the sixteenth percentile. His score on socialization skills in particular, was at the 0.5th percentile. In other words, his socialization skills were virtually nonexistent. The school psychologist, who was part of the evaluation team, strongly suggested to us that we place Nicholas on medication to address his anxiety and aggressive behaviors. We flatly refused this suggestion. I couldn't, at the time, imagine giving psychotropic drugs to a three year old!

Nicholas easily qualified for speech and occupational therapy at the preschool program he began in September 1999. He had some difficulties adjusting to preschool. Because of his heightened anxiety over other children, his teachers had to place Nicholas's chair at the farthest corner of the classroom. Otherwise, he would not even enter the room, much less be able to attend to story time or receive his therapy. For months, he sat in the corner, during circle time, during snack time, despite the fact that there were only five other children in his class, all of whom were relatively quiet and gentle. Playtime was particularly troublesome, since it required him to move about the room and interact with the other children. Nicholas didn't know how to play with ordinary toys in an appropriate way, and certainly didn't know how to play with another child.

As Donald and I continued to wait for our appointment at Children's Hospital, I threw myself into more autism research. (I would soon find that this would become a relentlessly ongoing endeavor.) I had found some intriguing articles that suggested a link between mercury exposure and autism. During the previous few years, I myself had been in poor health, and had had several tests performed. One of them showed a high level of mercury in my blood. My doctor told me that mercury is a neurotoxic metal, and that it's found in fish, dental amalgams, and in childhood vaccinations. I had eaten fish frequently throughout my life and including my pregnancy with Nicholas. I also had a mouthful of dental amalgams. I had spent the better part of that previous year

undergoing the removal/replacement of my amalgams, and eventually underwent chelation therapy, which removes the mercury
from the body. My health soon returned, and I had given up
eating fish for good. As I was reading these articles about mercury
and autism, I was starting to put the pieces together that perhaps
mercury was at least partially to blame for my son's condition.

In the early fall of 1999, Nicholas was tested for heavy
metals via hair analysis, by the same doctor who had treated me for
mercury toxicity. Nicholas's results for mercury were nearly off the
charts! Our doctor concluded that he received this mercury from
me, in utero, as well as through his childhood vaccinations. He
immediately underwent the same chelation protocol that I had
had, using dimercaptosuccinic acid (DMSA), the chelation drug
of choice in those days. He managed this treatment well, with no
negative side effects.

I have learned since that time, that besides being a powerful
neurotoxin, mercury is also implicated in a myriad of intestinal
and biochemical disturbances that often plague autistic children,
such as yeast and bacterial overgrowths, leaky gut, and in turn,
food sensitivities/allergies, particularly to gluten and casein-based
foods. It would be years later before I would come to fully realize
how many of Nicholas's autistic symptoms were very likely corre-
lated to his toxic exposure to mercury. We were fortunate to have
had Nicholas undergo mercury chelation as the *first* major intervention we tried. There is evidence today that indicates that the
presence of mercury impedes the effectiveness of many other
treatments, such as vitamins, minerals or other supplements, and
other educational/therapeutic interventions.

About a year after Nicholas began his DMSA treatments, we
learned that his mercury levels were nearly imperceptible!

Also during the fall of 1999, I had the good fortune of

attending an autism conference that was suggested to me by Nicholas's speech therapist. The conference was about auditory integration training (AIT), with Annabel Stehli as the featured speaker. I was captivated by her personal and compelling story about her own daughter's struggle with autism, and her amazing recovery, as a result of the sound therapy called AIT. I learned about the concept of "hearing equals behavior," and learned that a significant number of children with autism have painful hearing. And this pain causes many of these children to act out aggressively. It hinders their ability to hear sounds properly, resulting in poor language skills. Along with sensitive hearing, many of these children also suffer from hyperacusis, which is the ability to hear sounds at decibel levels that are ordinarily inaudible to the human ear. Or as I eventually would call it, "bionic" hearing. Every example that Annabel had described about her daughter's sound sensitivities struck a resounding chord with our own son's experiences. Could it be that Nicholas had this condition? As I recalled in my mind the numerous times I'd find Nicholas covering his ears over very ordinary sounds, the times he could hear a fire truck siren many seconds before anyone else could, and of course, all his aggressive behavior, it surely seemed so.

I went home from that conference very intrigued by this concept of sensitive hearing. Could this really explain many if not most of Nicholas's odd behaviors? I decided to try an experiment. One afternoon, Nicholas was watching one of his favorite "Thomas" videos, and as usual, he had covered his ears. I sat behind Nicholas so that he could not see me, and I decided to press the "mute" button on the remote control. I then watched him as he slowly lowered his hands from his ears as he turned to look back at me. His facial expression was one mixed with equal parts of relief and awe. Making full eye contact, he then uttered a breathy, "thank you." I muffled a gasp. "It's true!" I thought to myself. Oh my gosh, it's true. Tears fell down my cheeks, as I watched him turn back to contentedly watch his silent video. It was all becoming very clear to me. Scenes of Nicholas's previous behaviors flashed through my mind rapidly. The time Nicholas punched Donald in the face when he merely said, "good morning." The time he threw a tantrum when I had simply slid a chair under the table. All the times he pummeled his baby brother, just because he was babbling. Nicholas wasn't behaving as an angry, aggressive, cruel child because that was his nature. No, he behaved that way because that was the only way he could express his pain! Daddy's voice, moving chairs, his brother's nearly constant chattiness, certain videos, children's squeals, and all the sounds that no one else could hear, but he surely could — it was all driving him to madness!

Now that we knew that our son was living a tortured life of sound, we wanted Nicholas to have this sound therapy as soon as possible. That night, we contacted Annabel Stehli, to help us locate an AIT practitioner that was perhaps somewhere near where Donald's parents lived in Pennsylvania, since there wasn't one in our area. She told us there was one in King of Prussia. Our mouths dropped open, for that is the very town Donald's parents lived in! We took this as a sign from God, that we were on the right track on our quest to help our son. Since this therapy is a ten-day treatment, we chose our appointment for the following April, to coincide with the Easter break. It would be a long wait, but we reassured ourselves with the hope that help was on the way.

Christmas and Nicholas's fourth birthday came suddenly upon us. Staring blankly at his birthday cake, Nicholas didn't seem to be aware of what it was for. His vacant look, and silence, were a stark contrast to last year's birthday celebration, when he was so animated, so happy. Our home life now was better described as an "insane asylum," as I would sometimes call it. At four years old, he was still having tantrums nearly every day. His screams of distress and opposition were tiring to hear and to cope with. His bouts with aggression were an ever-present threat. I was at times literally afraid of my own son. He was bigger now, and strong. Despite his prowess, I still needed to spoon/fork-feed him, pick up his sandwiches to place in his mouth to eat, and I still needed to dress him.

Because of his significant delays in self-help skills, we enlisted the services of a private occupational therapist (OT), whom he saw twice a week at the local hospital, in addition to what he was receiving at his preschool. This OT provided Nicholas with the much needed sensory integration therapy, to address his many tactile and visual sensitivities, as well as provide him with opportunities to gain better gross and fine motor skills. Nicholas did make some good progress with this approach. He soon became less stressed out over the sensation of clothing on his skin, although I still needed to cut the tags off the back of all his shirts. I considered this a minor victory!

⸺⸺

Late January 2000, our appointment with the autism specialist at Children's Hospital was finally upon us. Nicholas first underwent a two-hour evaluation by a testing specialist. We sat in with Nicholas during these tests. He seemed to be doing well on the picture identification parts of test, and some of the other visually oriented tasks. But during the oral part of the evaluation, Nicholas had great difficulty. Nicholas was shown a picture of an umbrella, and he was asked to identify it. Nicholas quickly answered, "Umbrella." Then the psychometrist asked him, "Now Nicholas, when do you need to use an umbrella?" Nicholas stared at the wall behind the man, and paused a great while. He had no reply. Picture after picture, question after question, it was all the same. He knew what the objects were called, but could not answer what they were used for. Even with "simpler" questions such as, "Name me an animal," he still couldn't come up with an answer. And I knew he knew what animals were! After an hour and a half of this kind of testing, the psychometrist paused, and looked directly at Donald and I and said, with a half-laugh, "This kid doesn't comprehend anything!" There was nothing funny about it, I thought to myself. And I just wanted to grab Nicholas and run out that room that instant! Wasn't it already painful enough for us to have to watch our son perform so poorly on so many of these tests?

Finally it was our turn to meet with the autism specialist, Dr. Melinda Bellows. While she reviewed Nicholas's test results and other reports, Nicholas went off to the corner of the office to look at the toys that were there. Dr. Bellows smiled softly as she explained Nicholas's test results to us, and what they indicated. She occasionally would glance Nicholas's way while speaking with us. At one point she observed that Nicholas had not, during all the time that we were in her office, made any attempt to engage with her, or even look her way. In fact, she noted that Nicholas had not even made any contact with either of us. Regrettably it was true.

At last she announced, "Nicholas qualifies for the diagnosis of autism." I asked her, "Does he really have autism, or is it really Asperger's syndrome?" She explained that his diagnosis was true autism, since Nicholas had had a language delay, and delays in other areas, and those kinds of delays are not typically associated with the diagnosis of Asperger's.

"Well," I went on, "is he at least high-functioning?"

"Well," she paused, "he does have cognitive function. So, yes, I guess you could say that he's high-functioning."

"Cognitive function," I muttered to myself. It sounded so clinical. As if she were merely stating that he had at least had brain activity. Then she offered, "I can see that this diagnosis is troubling you. But you need to realize that Nicholas is the same boy now as the one you walked in here with this morning."

Yes, that was true. But oh, it sure didn't feel like it. I felt like my heart was breaking once again. Oh sure, I had suspected for these past six months that he probably had autism. Our lives had certainly been turned upside down this past year. But somehow, this "official" pronouncement of autism made it so real, so final, so inescapable. I looked down at my Nicholas, as he fumbled aimlessly with the toys, and it was as if I was looking at him for the very first time. With new eyes. And I realized in that moment that I really didn't know him at all. And whatever perceptions I may have ever had about him were completely washed away that afternoon. It was finally time for me to let go of my idealized picture of my son, something I thought I had done six months ago, but now realized I truly hadn't. And it was time for me to begin to get to know the "real" Nicholas. We left Children's Hospital with nothing more than a diagnosis in our hands, and with the only advice from the doctor being continued special education and, of course, medication.

The remaining winter months went on in much the same fashion as the fall. There were some small victories along the way. His teachers told me that Nicholas was now sitting with the rest of his classmates during story and snack times, as long as they placed an empty chair on either side of him. "Well, that's progress!" I thought. And Nicholas was starting to pick up some food items to feed himself, due to the sensory program he was receiving at the hospital. I welcomed any small gain.

However, his hostile behavior did not abate, nor did his frequent screaming. One morning, as I was seeing Nicholas off to the school bus, he climbed onto the bus with his ears covered. He chose a window seat that faced where I was standing. He looked straight at me, with his ears covered, and I could see him screaming, as if in torment. When the bus returned him home later that day, I had asked the aide on the bus if Nicholas was okay. She explained that he always screamed and covered his ears whenever a boy named John happened to be on the bus. I eventually learned that John squealed whenever the bus came to a stop. I knew immediately what the problem was. I thanked her for her time, and told her I would be driving Nicholas to school from then on. She gave me a puzzled look, but I knew I needed to spare Nicholas, what was for him, an unbearable situation. Even though I was now driving him to school every day, Nicholas was still so frightened of this boy's squeals that he would cover his ears whenever he saw John's bus arriving in the school parking lot, even if we were still inside our car! It is remarkable how traumatizing life must be for those with severe sound sensitivity. The use of medication was starting to sound good to me about now, if not for Nicholas, at least for me! I was in such despair over Nicholas's behaviors, and his many difficulties. I actually heard myself say to Donald one day, "If AIT doesn't fix this sensitive hearing and his aggressiveness, then let's medicate him. I can't handle this anymore, and neither can Nicholas." I prayed I would not have to eat my words. April couldn't come soon enough for us.

April finally arrived. As they lived nearly a thousand miles away in Florida, my parents, God bless them, wanted to help us in some way, so they paid for all four of our plane fares to Philadelphia. They didn't really understand this whole AIT idea, but who could blame them? It sounded a bit wacky to me too. I mean, just listening to some strangely altered music twice a day for ten days is going to "fix" somebody's ears?! We were all operating on a good measure of faith during those days. Donald and I had considered it interesting that Nicholas's AIT sessions were to begin on Good Friday, during this Easter break. We considered it another sign, and clung to the hope that this treatment would bring about a real start to his recovery, a "resurrection" of sorts. (And coincidentally, or perhaps not so, I happen to be writing this portion of Nicholas's story, also in April, on the eve of Good Friday.)

Nicholas was in pretty bad shape the day we arrived in Pennsylvania, with us having had a flight delay and with him not having slept well the night before. Nicholas had brought his typical "bad attitude" with him. His usual behavior of hitting himself, his brother, and Daddy; screaming "No!"; and his general uncooperative and oppositional behavior were all in full force. We were really discouraged, even though we had long been accustomed to this behavior.

Our first stop was at the audiologist's office, for the required audiogram. He would not cooperate with the audiologist at all. In fact all he did was cry and cover his ears. He would not wear the headphones, and would not (or could not), follow the audiologist's instructions. She eventually tried a different tactic. While Nicholas sat on my lap in the sound booth, and without headphones on, the audiologist decided to simply whisper some questions to Nicholas. Actually, I couldn't hear her at all, but I noticed Nicholas occasionally nodding, or shaking his head, and sometimes providing "answers" such as "blue" or "five." After ten minutes of this, the audiologist turned her speaker up to explain to me that she had just been asking Nicholas a variety of questions, at a whispered voice that measured between -10 and -20 decibels, inaudible to most. It was little wonder I could not hear what she was asking Nicholas, but *he* certainly could! This experiment gave the audiologist enough information to chart out an audiogram that the AIT practitioner could find useful.

Then we set out to the AIT practitioner. A young and friendly woman, Dena Farbman, welcomed us in, and set up her equipment. Nicholas once again refused to wear the headphones. But we snuck them on him, and as soon as he heard the music, he calmed down and began playing with his Play-Doh. In thirty minutes it was done, and we returned to Donald's parents' house. Five hours later, we returned to Dena's office for the second session of the day. This time, he didn't even want to go into the room, much less wear the headphones. But again, as soon as he heard the music, he calmed down. He seemed to enjoy it, although it was hard to tell what he was thinking. He was still very much in his own world, and as with the first session, he didn't look at anyone the whole time. Right after the session, Dena took his headphones off. He looked at her and asked, "What's your name?" And she replied with her name. Then Nicholas asked her, "Oh, how old are you?" She said with a laugh, "Twenty," for she was not that young! Then he turned to Donald and said, "How old are you, Dad?" We were simply stunned. This was the first time that we had ever heard him try to carry on a conversation with anyone that didn't involve him asking for food or a drink. It was then time for us to leave, but Nicholas didn't want to go! Dena had another client waiting, so we coaxed him out the door. While we walked out, Nicholas said he wanted to come back tomorrow! We drove to Donald's parents' house with tears in our eyes.

The next several days' sessions went smoothly from then out. While Nicholas had his headphones on, playing mindlessly with his Play-Doh, we chatted with Dena, who happened to also work exclusively with autistic children as a behaviorist. From her observations, she told us that Nicholas was the most auditorally hypersensitive child she had ever seen in her practice. That actually was of some comfort to hear. When we asked her when we would start to see improvements in his hearing sensitivities, she said that many children start to show an improvement on day seven of this ten-day treatment. "magic day seven," she liked to call it.

While we waited for this "magical" day, Nicholas's behavior continued on much as it had always been. Still lots of hostility, both physical and verbal, toward Anthony and his father, and lots of hitting himself in the face and head. Our visit at his grandparents' house was unpleasant for them, to say the least. By this point in our two-week stay, they were beginning to fully realize how angry a young man our son was. Even during one of the AIT sessions, Nicholas hit himself, when Donald merely *looked* at him! And of course, Nicholas was still covering his ears during certain parts of his cartoon videos, as well as many other sounds.

On day seven, on our way to his first AIT of the day, Nicholas was in rare form, growling at everyone, uncooperative, and hitting himself. But after the session, Nicholas seemed to be in a significantly better frame of mind. When we returned to his grandparents' house, he said cheerfully, "Hi, Mom-mom!" My mother-in-law spun around in surprise, since this was the first time he had greeted her since our arrival over a week ago! He was also less aggressive toward Anthony that day, and seemed more in control emotionally. In the afternoon, Nicholas was playing in the basement with his grandfather. When I called down to him that it was time to come upstairs for dinner, there was no verbal or physical protest, as there usually would have been. He just bounded up the stairs happily. During that day's second AIT session, instead of his usual burying of his head and hands playing with Play-Doh, Nicholas instead looked around the room, as if noticing it for the first time. He began investigating all the toys that Dena had had in her office. He saw a small bean bag that he decided he wanted to toss across the room to daddy. Donald tossed it back to him, and Nicholas threw it back once more. Nicholas began smiling, and soon, he was laughing! This tossing game went on for a few minutes, when he decided to throw the beanbag to me, and eventually to Dena. So for nearly a half hour, the four of us were engaged in this delightful game of toss! He was, for the first time, making good eye contact and fully engaged with those around him, in a positive exchange, and to his own delight. Donald and I could barely remember the last time we had seen him laugh, and with such joy.

Later that evening, Anthony had fallen down in the living room, and started crying. Nicholas did not scream or hit himself (as was typical), and he even went up to Anthony to stroke his hair lovingly! He told him he was sorry for pushing him, even though he had not in fact pushed him down. It was a stunning display of empathy, that we had not seen from him ever before.

The next morning, Anthony greeted Nicholas with a cheerful "Good morning." This was usually met with growls, protests or pushing. But instead, I heard Nicholas say nicely and calmly, "Good morning, Anthony." When I handed Nicholas his breakfast toast, he said to me, "Thank you, Mommy." I nearly fell over. After breakfast, I found Nicholas and Anthony sitting next to each other watching a video together. Normally, Nicholas would always need or want to be seated alone on the couch.

With so many of these wonderful changes, something was certainly different about Nicholas, ever since yesterday, I thought to myself. Yes, yesterday was "magic day seven." Could it be that Nicholas is truly responding to AIT as we had all hoped he would? Looking back, that day heralded the turning point in all of our lives as a family. It would become the day that Nicholas was literally being set free, released from his prison of tortured sound, and awakening to the world around him.

As the AIT sessions drew to a close, it became very clear to us that Nicholas was certainly benefiting from this intervention. Oh, things weren't perfect by a long shot, but we were at least seeing significant positive changes in him, which led us to believe that better days were coming. Nicholas was beginning to let us hug and kiss him at bedtime now, something he fully resisted before. He was calmer, less anxious, and less aggressive with his brother. We were so grateful that we had had the opportunity to provide our son with this vital treatment.

At the Philadelphia airport, on our way back home to Indiana, an interesting thing happened. There was an indoor children's playground in the terminal where we were waiting for our flight. There was a little girl there who was almost five and about the same size as Nicholas. She approached Nicholas and started playing and wrestling with him, even to the point of jumping on him and rolling on top of him and tickling him. And he loved it! He would then do the same to her. We watched those two in amazement. If anyone would have walked by and watched them, they would have thought that they were playing like brother and sister. Nicholas had always shied away from his peers, if not run away from them. But now, for the first time in his life, he was starting to enjoy the company of children. We knew in that moment, that we were surely flying home with a new Nicholas.

That first week back home was wonderful. When Nicholas talked to either of us now, he would look right up at us and make full and sustained eye contact while speaking. He returned a smile with a smile. He was starting to ask a lot of questions now, about how things work, and why does this or that happen. It was as if he was finally interested in the world around him, as well as caring about the people in his life. Once when he bumped into Anthony, and knocked him over, he said, "Sorry, that was my fault." He was beginning to be able to tell me, in words, when things were bothering him. One morning he said to me, "Mom, my back is hot. The sun is on my back." And he was right! His back was hot, because he had been sitting at the kitchen table with his back to the window, the sun beating down on him. While outside one day, Nicholas was finished riding his bike, and I saw him put his bike away all by himself. I heard him say to himself, "Oh, I should put my bike away." And he proceeded to drag it from the driveway back into the garage where it belonged! I was amazed! I was also beginning to notice that his facial skin color was looking "healthier," not as pale as he had always been, and that even his dark circles under his eyes were less noticeable. One evening right before bath time, I dared to ask Nicholas for a hug. He opened his arms, smiling, and jumped into my lap and embraced me as I hugged him tightly, kissing him all over. He kissed me back on my shoulder. He was actually happy to be in my arms. I cherished tearfully, the fact that I was holding my Nicholas again!

But soon, all would not be so rosy. Annabel Stehli and Dena Farbman both had advised us that Nicholas would experience "side effects" post-AIT, at fairly predictable intervals — at the one week, one month, and three months post-AIT time periods. Unfortunately, right on cue, those side effects began, exactly one week after his last day of AIT. That wonderful, blissful first week came crashing to an end. The outbursts, self-injury, and aggression toward Anthony all resurfaced. It was devastating to see these terrible behaviors return, after having had a nice good break from them all. I personally found it more difficult to cope with these behaviors now, than before the AIT. Now that I knew what Nicholas could really be like, I disdained those old behaviors all the more. Fortunately, this regression only lasted three days, but it had felt like an eternity. It was so good to see the "new" Nicholas return to us again.

As the weeks passed, we were finding that Nicholas was becoming more "teachable." He was now more open to our verbal correction and instruction for better behavior. It was almost as if we had to begin anew in teaching him the proper way to behave. (God knows we had tried all along!) But maybe now, and only now, was he really able to receive our instruction and learn from it, now that sounds, and particularly speech, were less painful and more understandable to him. We also noticed that Nicholas was less obsessive over his *Thomas the Tank Engine* trains, which he used to play with in an almost compulsive way. He hardly played with them now. And slowly over time, he began to trust that those sounds on certain videos didn't hurt him anymore. In just a few weeks, he began lowering his hands from his ears. At first, he would just hold them near his ears, sort of like, "just in case." But soon, he began realizing that he didn't need to do that anymore, and he eventually watched his videos without any anxiety at all. I don't think I will ever fully appreciate what an effort and leap of faith it must have taken for Nicholas to overcome this very real fear of sounds. I was (and am) so proud of him!

Those first few months after AIT were a continuing adventure for us, as we watched Nicholas blossom before our eyes. One day as I was driving Nicholas to school, Anthony, who was also in the car, was looking out the window and commenting on all the trucks we passed. Anthony's dialogue went something like this (spoken in his two-year-old extremely high-pitched and very loud voice): "Look at the truck!! There's a truck! Mommy, a truck!! I see it!! I see a truck! Nicky, I see a truck!!!" etc, etc. This went on for a few minutes. And instead of swatting Anthony over the head, as he would in the past, Nicholas just blithely said, almost under his breath, "Okay, Anthony, we get the point." I gasped in amazement, and then I couldn't stop laughing all the way to the school. Nicholas has a sense of humor! Even though I wasn't sure he knew it quite yet.

By midsummer, Nicholas was at the three-month mark, post-AIT, and that was by far, the worst side effect period. His behavior and cognitive abilities regressed to what he was like before AIT. This was a very difficult time for all of us, as we struggled through each day of living the "nightmare" over again. This regression lasted until early September, nearly two months. I had daily feared that this would never end, and that we had lost him again, and forever. But gratefully, as mysteriously as the regression began, it quietly lifted away. And although Nicholas still had had some lingering negative behavior issues after this troubling period of time, he would never again be found hitting himself in the head or attacking Anthony. He also no longer covered his ears over any particular sound. We considered these "milestones" a major victory!

Now that Nicholas's painful hearing was no longer an issue, we could see that he still had many more hurdles to overcome. During the summer, I learned through my continued autism research that many autism spectrum children are helped greatly by a biomedical approach. I read with great interest Dr. William Shaw's book, *Biological Treatments for Autism and PDD*. From this book I learned that many autistic children have very disturbed metabolisms, due to high levels of intestinal bacteria and yeast, as well as many other biochemical imbalances. And in Nicholas's case, primarily caused by his exposure to high levels of mercury. These imbalances, overgrowths, and sometimes deficiencies all can contribute to poor behavioral and cognitive functioning, particularly in the autism population. This book soon became my autism

"Bible." We eventually had Nicholas undergo several of the medical tests suggested in the book, and found that Nicholas indeed had elevated levels of certain harmful bacteria and yeast in his intestinal system. We then began introducing several supplements into Nicholas's diet, to address these harmful overgrowths, as well as adding supplements that were shown to increase overall function in autistic children. After MUCH trial and error during the following year, we discovered these supplements that brought about the best changes during this point in Nicholas's life: culturelle (a probiotic that controls bacterial and yeast overgrowth), dimethylaminoethanol (DMAE), a neurotransmitter; omega-3 essential fatty acids, i.e., docosahexaenoic acid (DHA) and elcosapentaenoic acid (EPA) (for overall brain and eye functioning); trimethylglicene (TMG) with folic acid and Vitamin B-12; and extra calcium and magnesium, since he had shown a deficiency in these two important minerals.

While I was "experimenting" with my newfound knowledge of biological testing and supplement usage, Nicholas was beginning his second year of special education preschool. He was now able to ride the bus to school once again, and his adjustment to his new class and teacher went relatively smoothly. His behavior at home and in the classroom, although much improved over the past several months, still needed some fine-tuning. His physical aggression was becoming under control, but Nicholas still had many problems with managing his frustrations. And he was frustrated easily! Assembling his train tracks, building with his Legos, dressing himself, feeding himself, etc., were all experiences that could potentially set off a tirade of screams and angry outbursts. If we tried to intercede to help him, this would only anger him further.

Nicholas's overall behavior was "choppy" at best, with lots of ups and downs, good moments mixed with bad ones. One afternoon I took both boys to the playground for the first time in months. Nicholas was playing so well around and with the other children, and really having a good time and enjoying himself. A far cry from a year ago, when he would just run away in fear. But all of a sudden, he started crying, and then howling like a wolf, his neck craned up towards the sky. He was having a meltdown because Anthony didn't want to follow him. (Nicholas always needed things to go just his way.) All of the other parents stared at him perplexed, and I just ignored it (or least tried to), and he eventually stopped the wolf act. Then suddenly, he resumed playing nicely again, as if nothing at all had happened. Flashes of brilliance, mixed in with insanity, I thought to myself.

This odd pattern of up and down behavior, good signs mixed with bad, continued for several more months. On the one hand, we'd be celebrating over Nicholas as he expanded his choice of foods he'd eat, and his starting to read, and his increased imaginative play. These were all very good signs of progress. But on the other hand, Nicholas's speech was sometimes extremely illogical. One evening at bedtime, Nicholas said this to Donald (as recorded in my journal): "Daddy, let's talk about Jesus's life. The Bible was mad at life and God because he had to go to the store. So now you know. But I don't think that I have my trains and Anthony fell down, but I can do it all by myself, but the Bible said Jesus made God and mommy was going to bed and so I think so, ok?" We were glad to be hearing his voice on a regular basis now, but we had no idea what he was really trying to say.

There were other times when Nicholas had made very earnest attempts at communicating his thoughts, but again, with great difficulty. On another evening at bedtime, Nicholas was excitedly pointing to the Bible story that Donald was reading. He said, "Daddy, oh Daddy, I have a question!" We then watched

Nicholas move his mouth open and closed repeatedly, almost as if he were hiccuping, but no words were coming out. Then, after much more silent mouth moving, he said somberly, "Uh, I can't. It's too hard." Donald continued on with the story, and after several more minutes, Nicholas was finally able to ask his question. He had wanted to know what a certain word was in the story, that's all. Such a simple request really, but for him, it had been such a struggle. He had had an idea in his mind, couldn't retrieve it, and therefore couldn't express it. What was sadder still, is that we could see that Nicholas was now consciously aware that he was having problems expressing himself. And this could only further add to his ever-mounting frustrations.

It was about this time that a neighbor of ours introduced us to an educational/therapeutic intervention called the neurodevelopmental approach. The thinking behind this approach, as it relates to autism, is based largely on the work of Carl Delacato, among others, and is discussed in fuller detail in his book, *The Ultimate Stranger.* Basically, the neurodevelopmental approach is based on the concepts that the brain is organized in a hierarchical manner, and that the brain is "plastic," meaning that it is highly adaptable and therefore can change its structure, function, and chemistry, when provided with specific stimulation and input. Coming from a psychology background, I found this body of study fascinating. But mostly, I found it to be so utterly logical. I knew that my son had many sensory issues that had affected his hearing, vision, and senses of touch and smell. I also knew that Nicholas was very clumsy, had poor fine and gross motor skills. And most of all, I knew how troubling his illogical speech was to him and everyone around him.

Although Nicholas had been receiving several types of interventions during the past year or so, I was beginning to believe that something was missing in our approach. As I kept reading about the neurodevelopmental approach, I learned that this intervention employed all of the other separate therapeutic modalities (i.e., speech therapy, occupational therapy, sensory integration, biomedical, etc.) into one cohesively integrated approach, and in a neurologically organized fashion, based on how the brain actually develops and works. After much prayer and reflection, Donald and I believed that this was perhaps the missing piece to Nicholas's continued recovery, and decided to pursue this approach.

In February 2001, we set out for Dayton, Ohio, for Nicholas's first neurodevelopmental (ND) evaluation, with Cyndi Ringoen, a neurodevelopmentalist certified through the International Association of Christian NeuroDevelopmentalists (ICAN). Mrs. Ringoen looked over Nicholas's history inventory and spent about an hour evaluating him. She assessed his fine and gross motor abilities, expressive language, visual and auditory systems, and his tactility. She also assessed his math and reading skills. After the hour evaluation, we sat and discussed his results. She explained to us that Nicholas's gross motors skills were delayed at the toddler stage of development, and his tactile sensitivities were quite significant. Academically however, he tested at the middle of the first grade in both reading and math skills. She told us Nicholas was quite bright, and that once we addressed his motor skills and tactility, that he should do quite well. During the past almost two years, this was the first time a professional had ever said anything positive and hopeful to us about our son's condition and prognosis.

After we finished our discussion with Mrs. Ringoen, she wrote up an ND program for Nicholas. This was a tailor-made program of exercises and activities that we would do with Nicholas, several hours a day, five to six days a week, for the next four months, until his follow-up evaluation in June. These exercises and activities included such things as cross creeping and crawling, rubbing his skin with tactile gloves, deep pressure, vision and auditory exercises, hand strengthening exercises, among many other things. They were chosen to specifically address and meet Nicholas's unique needs, according to his particular developmental profile. She also added math and reading activities to his program, since he was showing strong abilities in these areas. I spent the next hour of our appointment being trained by her assistant on how to do each of these program activities, so that I could execute his program on my own, at home. I wasn't sure I would feel confident enough to do a program like this, but after the hour's training, along with the friendly support we had received by Mrs. Ringoen and her staff, I felt much more at ease. When we were done with the training, we drove back to Indiana, with a new bag of "tools" in our hands!

I was excited to begin this new intervention. I wasn't sure how I was going to fit all these new activities into our day, since Nicholas was still attending preschool for half a day. But after a month or so, it almost seemed as if we always had been doing this. Part of the reason for this is that the ND program often felt like drudgery! For five to six days a week, we did the same activities every day. Some were fun for Nicholas, some were challenging. Some he resisted doing at first. It was an adjustment period for all of us. But soon, we started seeing some real changes.

About two to three months after beginning his ND program, Nicholas's short-term memory was significantly improved, as a direct result of one of his ND exercises. Prior to this program, if we would ever have given Nicholas a two-step direction, he would either do the first step, or the second step, but he would not remember both steps. He just couldn't process that much information at one time, and then carry it out. This increase in his short-term memory also spilled over into his receptive and expressive language. In the past, he would falter and hesitate, first with trying to fully understand what was being asked of him, and then with struggling to find the word or words he wanted to say. This became noticeably reduced. He was now speaking with better fluency, and using appropriate words to express his thoughts and replies. And in turn, with the increase in receptive and expressive language ability, his episodes of frustration were also decreasing. As I watched this "ripple effect" stemming from just one of the ND exercises, I marveled over the beauty and simplicity of this approach. Yes, the brain can do marvelous things, given the right input, with the right amount of intensity and duration. It was almost as if I were watching Nicholas's brain being "rewired." And in fact, it truly was.

During this four-month period while I was busy with Nicholas's ND program, Donald had found a new job in New Jersey. The boys and I stayed behind in Indiana for a time, until our house was sold, and we rejoined Donald in New Jersey in early June. Despite the tumult that a cross-country move usually entails, Nicholas handled these significant changes in our lives with relative ease. I continued with his ND program, no matter where we happened to be. On the plane, at the hotel, and in the apartment where we lived temporarily. This program was actually the only constant in our lives, during those chaotic days of relocating and eventually unpacking and settling into our new home. I honestly believe that Nicholas would not have managed this move as well as he had, had it not been for his ND program. It gave order and structure to our days, and it kept his progress on track, despite his now being out of school, and receiving no other special needs services. I surely expected a regression of some kind during this transition. It never happened. In fact, he only continued to improve.

In late June, it was time for Nicholas's follow-up ND evaluation. Since Cyndi Ringoen did not see clients as far east as New Jersey, we were reassigned to another neurodevelopmentalist, Mrs. Linda Kane. She was located in Annapolis, Maryland, a two and a half hour drive from our new home. We were eager to see how much Nicholas had progressed since February. As with his initial evaluation, Nicholas was assessed on all the previous parameters for an hour by Linda Kane. She told us that Nicholas had made some gains in his gross motor skills, as well as his visual perception. He had gained five months in his math skills, and gained an entire grade year plus two months in his reading skills! But Nicholas still had some major issues in his tactility profile, and we had some concerns about some of his lingering negative behaviors. Mrs. Kane wanted to also address his immature social conversational skills as well as his reading comprehension skills. She then wrote up a revised ND program for him that included exercises that specifically addressed his deficiencies at this point. I was then trained by her assistant in the new activities in his program. All in all, it felt great to see objective evidence of Nicholas's progress, and to have a new set of exercises to work on, to bring about further development.

Two weeks later, Nicholas was evaluated by the child study team in our local school district, in order to determine placement in kindergarten that fall. He once again went through an exhaustive battery of tests, (psychological, occupational therapy, speech and language, and academic). At the assessment review meeting, we were told that Nicholas could be mainstreamed into a regular kindergarten classroom! Although he did fairly well on most areas of the testing, particularly academics, Nicholas was still weak in pragmatic (social language) speech, and had some fine motor delays. Because of these issues, he still qualified for speech and occupational therapy. His case manager, Evelyn Saunders, who was also the school psychologist, also recommended that we consider placing Nicholas on medication, to reduce his hyperactivity and distractibility, and to help increase his focus and frustration tolerance. At this point in our lives, this oft repeated suggestion was becoming downright comical! Yes, I was aware that Nicholas still had some unresolved issues in these areas, but once again, I politely refused this suggestion. I knew I now had the tools to help Nicholas overcome these remaining disabilities. It was just going to take a little bit longer to achieve than the quick fix found in a small white pill. Mrs. Saunders continued to urge us in the use of medication, citing her concerns over Nicholas's ability to handle a large group regular education setting. We remained firm and declined this suggestion. Because of this, Mrs. Saunders then recommended that Nicholas be assigned an aide to work with him in the classroom. It was a generous offer, and we gratefully accepted this arrangement. We left the assessment meeting ecstatic that Nicholas had at least been mainstreamed, and we looked forward to September full of renewed hope.

As we awaited the start of the new school year, I spent the summer months settling into our new home, continuing Nicholas's ND and nutritional supplement programs, and as always, reading and researching the latest news about autism. In an autism newsletter I had subscribed to, I came across a research study involving the use of digestive enzymes that were shown to bring about very significant improvements in autistic children. The enzymes used in this study, peptizyde and HN-zyme prime, were developed in response to earlier research indicating that many children on the autism spectrum lacked certain digestive enzymes needed in order to break down the peptides produced by proteins found in wheat and dairy products. It has been speculated that these undigested proteins and peptides in turn cause some of the undesirable autistic behaviors. According to this study's report, after four months on the enzymes, the children showed significant improvements in eye contact, language, humor, sleep, transitioning, socialization, awareness, problem solving, short-term memory, flexibility in routine, range of interests, sensory integration, spontaneous affection, among many other measures. Significant decreases were seen in aggression, hyperactivity, anxiety, self-stimulating and self-injurious behaviors, among others. It was also noted that the children became noticeably more pleasant, easygoing, cooperative, and helpful.

The results cited in this study were simply too compelling for me to ignore. Although Nicholas had never before appeared to have any obvious digestive problems or sensitivities to certain foods, most of the areas of improvement reported in this study were issues Nicholas still needed work on. I wasn't sure if these enzymes could help Nicholas, but after doing a bit more research and discussing it with Donald, I decided to order these digestive enzymes and give them a try. I felt we had nothing to lose.

Nicholas began taking the enzymes just days before his first day of kindergarten. As advised by the manufacturer, I gave Nicholas only one capsule of each enzyme at only one meal a day, for the first few days. Then gradually we could add them to all the other meals. I'll never forget how Nicholas responded after his very first dose, taken at lunchtime. Within ten minutes, Nicholas began talking up a storm! He was suddenly very happy and animated. During our afternoon ND program activities, he was performing better on these exercises than I had ever seen. His voice was even better modulated. When Donald came home from work later that afternoon, Nicholas asked him to do something for him. Donald told him it would have to wait until after dinner, to which

Nicholas replied, "Okay Daddy, I'll be patient." This coming from a child who had always needed to have things go his way, right away! I had never expected to see such pronounced changes in him so soon.

After dinner, Nicholas, as if a switch had been turned off, suddenly became very oppositional and grumpy. I recalled what he had eaten for dinner, and realized it was pasta, a wheat-based food. And he had not had any enzymes at this meal, due to our needing to introduce them slowly. It then became very clear to me that Nicholas must indeed be having difficulty in digesting certain foods, and that that in turn was causing such disagreeable behavior. In the days that followed, this same pattern showed up. Pleasant and agreeable while on the enzymes, a miserable tyrant without them. I now had all the proof I needed. Nicholas needed these enzymes!

Within two weeks, Nicholas was taking the full dose of enzymes with every meal. And his overall attitude, behavior, and speech just continued to blossom and remained steady throughout the day. Fortunately, this coincided with his first days and weeks at school. He thoroughly enjoyed his new school and class. His teacher and aide either called me or wrote me notes nearly every day those first few weeks, telling me how wonderfully Nicholas was doing at school. Nicholas was making friends in his class and on the bus, jumping off the school bus happy and smiling, and excitedly telling me all about his day. I was so happy and proud knowing that Nicholas was making this very big adjustment to regular school so well.

Not two weeks of school passed when Evelyn Saunders, Nicholas's case manager, called me at home one day during school hours. She called to share with me her observations of Nicholas on one of her recent visits to his classroom.

"Mrs. Damiani, I have to tell you that your son is the happiest and most well-behaved child in his class," she began. "When it's time to line up for the bus, all the other kids are restless and poking each other and not paying attention. But not Nicholas. He just calmly stands in line, not fidgeting or bothering anyone. At sharing time today, I watched as Nicholas attentively listened to one his classmates sharing about her new coat. When the teacher asked the class if anyone had a question or comment for the girl, Nicholas raised his hand and kindly said, 'Rebecca, that is a very beautiful coat.'"

At this point I was already in tears, but Mrs. Saunders animatedly continued, "Nicholas is just smiling from ear to ear, all the school day. He is helpful to his classmates, finishes his worksheets quickly, and presents no behavior problems at all. Frankly," she paused, "I didn't quite expect Nicholas to adapt this well to the classroom setting, given what I had observed from him two months ago, during our assessment of him. As you know, I recommended to you that he be placed on medication. I fully expected to see some problems with hyperactivity, or focus, or disruptive behavior of some sort. I'm simply amazed that I'm not seeing any of that! "

My mouth had been hanging open during all of her report. I responded meekly with, "Oh, that's so nice to hear." Or something understated like that. I was in too much shock even to know what to say. But I knew in my heart what was primarily responsible for all these significantly good changes his case manager had been seeing in Nicholas. It was the enzymes, no doubt about it. And of course, I had never told Mrs. Saunders or anyone at the school about Nicholas taking these enzymes. And I never did.

Mrs. Saunders then went on to say that Nicholas didn't appear to be needing an aide after all. But since they already had one in place, and his aide and he were working out so well, they would continue with this arrangement. She actually told me that Nicholas's aide was spending more of her time helping some of the other children in his class!

After Mrs. Saunders had finished giving me her report, I thanked her for calling, and plopped down into my easy chair, with my mouth still wide open. Then a big smile broke out on my face, and tears welled up once again. "He's really okay!" I shouted out loud. "Nicholas is really going to be okay!" I dared utter it again. Just as with those first days after AIT, I was once again feeling a renewed sense of hope, that Nicholas was turning yet another corner on his recovery. It was one more tender moment to treasure in this mother's heart.

The following month, in October, it was time for Nicholas's reevaluation with his neurodevelopmentalist Linda Kane in Annapolis. We were all excited to see her again, and to tell her all about the changes we were seeing in Nicholas during this past month. But we decided not to say anything to her until after she had spent her hour assessing him. After she had finished with Nicholas, we went and sat down in her office. She appeared reflective, and remained silent until she had had our full attention. Shaking her head slowly back and forth, she announced, "This is an entirely different child from the one I saw four months ago." She paused while Donald and I just beamed! She then went on to tell us that Nicholas appeared less anxious, that his social language skills had improved, he followed her directions well, he was expressing his thoughts better, and had a better tonal quality to his voice. In addition, his math skills were now at 2.6 (the second grade, sixth month level), and his reading ability was at 3.9! But more amazing than that, his scores on his reading comprehension were a 3.4! (third grade, fourth month.) Mrs. Kane found this score particularly interesting because she had tried to administer this very same test to Nicholas in June, but he just couldn't do it. He could read the passages all right, but could not correctly answer the comprehension questions. She told us his score in June was actually zero, and she had decided not to tell us this back then, because she felt it might unduly upset us. The fact that he had now jumped over three grade levels in four months, from virtually nothing, was quite a testimony! It was then that we told her all about these new enzymes Nicholas had been taking. She agreed that something metabolic was going on with Nicholas, and that when things are balanced internally, that in turn makes all other interventions work more powerfully. We couldn't agree more!! We left Annapolis with another revised ND program for Nicholas, and our hearts bursting with joy.

Nicholas continued to blossom during the remaining fall months, as well as overcome several more quirks. Getting a haircut had always been an ordeal for Nicholas. Lots of fussing and screaming. His sensitivity to touch had always been quite severe. But this one autumn day, we took him for his monthly haircut, and no screaming! He just calmly sat in the chair and let the hairdresser wet and cut his hair, as if nothing at all was the matter! I'm not sure who was more stunned in that moment, our hairdresser or us! "Look Daddy," Nicholas said, "this doesn't bother me anymore!" All those ND tactile exercises were starting to pay off! Nicholas was also becoming less afraid of trying new foods. Well, new foods for him, anyway. He started trying hardboiled eggs, raw carrots, meatballs, and even trying different drinks. And most of these new foods and drinks he actually liked!

With all of the positive changes we were seeing in Nicholas during this time, I do not mean to suggest that he never had another bad day again. As with any child recovering from autism,

Nicholas would experience occasional episodes of regression. These were periods of time when he would lose many of the gains he had made, and relapse into some his former autistic behaviors. These regressions would sometimes last only hours, or sometimes days, or very rarely, several weeks. And they would, almost without exception, be triggered by either an oncoming illness, an erupting tooth, a change in one of his nutritional supplements, or sometimes during the rare occasion when we took an extended break from the ND program (holidays, vacations, for example). Like any mother I suppose, I have always found it difficult to cope with any regressions, even though I knew that they were an unavoidable phase of my son's ongoing development. I had always wished that recovering from autism could just occur in a nice, neat package, of uninterrupted, linear progress. But alas, it is not so. Yet progress does occur (and is still occurring), despite the occasional and temporary setbacks. And as Nicholas has matured, his regressions have become less frequent, occurring with less severity and duration. That in itself has been an encouraging sign.

As Nicholas's kindergarten year continued into the late autumn, Evelyn Saunders had telephoned me again. She called to say once again how well Nicholas was doing at school, so much so, that she and his teacher had decided to recommend Nicholas to their school's gifted program! I was a little perplexed by this recommendation.

"Mrs. Saunders, how can Nicholas be considered for the gifted program, when he has a diagnosis of autism?" I asked. That's when Mrs. Saunders said something I never would have expected.

"Well, Mrs. Damiani, I've been meaning to talk to you about that. You see, I've been observing Nicholas during the past couple of months, while in his classroom, as well as while he's at his specials like art, music, and gym. He has been doing well, in all areas, in all situations. I'd really like for you to get Nicholas reevaluated. As a school psychologist, I've had the opportunity to observe lots of children on the autism spectrum. But from all that I'm seeing from Nicholas lately, I don't think he qualifies for this diagnosis any longer. I mean, I've been watching him closely, and I just don't see it!" she exclaimed emphatically.

"Oh my," I heard myself say under my breath. Mrs. Saunders continued with, "I really would like to see that label removed from Nicholas's school records. I don't think it should be there, and I wouldn't want to see this label follow him throughout his school career."

Now I really had nothing left to say. How could I? She expressed every secretly held wish I had ever had for Nicholas, since our autism adventure began nearly three years ago. As strange as this might sound, I was just as stunned and overcome with emotion over hearing a professional state that my son probably wasn't autistic any longer, as I was when a professional had first announced that he in fact was!

And from that day on, to this very day, Donald and I have found ourselves in that odd but happy predicament of raising a child who has recovered from autism. Where do we now belong? In the world of autism, with all of its despair and exasperation? Or in the world of "normal"? Where we could somehow "pretend" that nothing at all is wrong, and quietly disappear into the fabric of ordinary life once again. Well, in those months and years since that late autumn day in 2001, we have lived in both worlds. Never feeling quite comfortable in either one of these worlds, but nonetheless, gingerly walking the tightrope between the two, desiring to bring hope to the one, and an increase in awareness and compassion to the other.

EPILOGUE

The remainder of Nicholas's kindergarten year brought more triumphs. According to teacher reports, his social skills continued to develop very well, as Nicholas made friends within his class. His OT services were eventually dropped, due to attaining mastery levels in all required areas. "His handwriting is the best in his class," his therapist would write on his final OT report. By the end of his kindergarten year, Nicholas's math abilities were at the 3.6 grade level, and his reading and comprehension scores were at the 4.8 and 4.1 grade levels, respectively.

As of this writing, Nicholas is currently finishing up the first grade. He is now homeschooled, in part because of his very accelerated learning ability, as well as his remarkable response to the ND program, still an integral part of our lives. As of his most recent ND evaluation, his math abilities were at the 5.0 grade level, and his reading and comprehension scores were at the 5. 9 and 5.3 grade levels, respectively.

Nicholas is now a self-controlled, cooperative, and enthusiastic young man. He and his younger brother are now the best of friends and play so well together that it often gets other people's attention. A far cry from the days when we had often feared he might fatally injure his brother. Besides his brother, Nicholas has several other friends from his church and homeschool groups, most of whom do not know of his previous diagnosis. He delights us daily with his humor, and his obvious talents in drawing and writing. He's told us recently that he wants to be an artist when he grows up, swim with dolphins one day, and, if he can't have a baby sister, he wants two daughters when he gets married!

But best of all, he is a happy child now. The once tormented, angry, aggressive little boy is now a pleasant, inquisitive, and well-mannered young man. It is truly an amazing transformation. His future, once dark and uncertain, is now full of promise and purpose.

PEYTON

———— ⊶⊷ ————

Chris Hilton

Peyton is an active, happy, and very determined five year old. Yet in the past several years, he has had to make his brain significantly rewire itself to recreate the pathways that most of us take for granted.

When Peyton's little brother was a baby, we encouraged him to say good night to Ryan. He was not able to say the word, so he created his own unique way — a gentle head butt (a touch between two foreheads). Now Peyton can clearly say "Good night, Ryan," but this nonverbal sign of love remains an evening tradition. Over the past five years, we have learned to be very creative in how we communicate with each other. It's truly wonderful to learn that regardless of whether you use words, signs, symbols, or gestures, you can convey so much meaning. It can be exhausting! However, we keep in mind that the desire to communicate and the ability to satisfy ones needs are the basis for intelligence.

Every time I watch Peyton give this gentle head butt, I can't help think what a remarkable head he has. We have discovered firsthand the miracles that can occur within the brain when you provide intensive interventions to help with the rewiring process. Peyton's story involves a little boy whose brain did not work the way it should — even at a microscopic level. The journey to help him recover has taken us near and far, into a world we didn't truly appreciate before we started. A place where there are many dedicated people that just want to help children recover and to succeed. Due to the severity of Peyton's medical case, we discovered we needed to surround him with a select community of dedicated individuals all contributing their special talents to help a little boy come back from something devastating. Along this journey, we have received help, support, and amazing contributions from so many incredible people. Not only does Peyton have a strong family behind him, but a team of more than twenty-five medical and developmental professionals who each help to address part of the problem. We have relied on these individuals, but it has truly been Peyton who is the hero of this tale. During the past five years, we have watched with amazement how he has worked so hard to make exceptional progress.

WHO IS PEYTON?

Peyton is a little guy who is always described as happy, affectionate, and active. One of Peyton's most endearing characteristics is his penchant to flirt. You know you're a true buddy of his when he has done his head tilt at you. It's usually a slight tilt of his head to encourage you to tilt your head likewise. The best part is the huge grin and glint in his eyes that goes along with it. It's his bluish-gray eyes, now covered by wire-rim glasses, which are my most favorite feature. Even during the worst phase of his illness, you could always see this spark in his eyes. We just know that there is so much potential inside of him, but our challenge is to help it come out.

He is tall for his age. His chestnut brown hair has sparkly red highlights, which usually include a few devil horns here and there. His giggle is infectious, the sound we strive to hear. Balls, cars, trains, and books are his favorite toys. He is a physical guy and loves to have wrestling and tickling time with his daddy. While outside, he prefers swimming, swinging, and making basketball shots with amazing aim. Adventures in the car or plane bring him great joy. We affectionately refer to him as the Energizer Bunny, because he rarely stops.

Peyton's primary source of entertainment is listening to music. He truly has brought a constant stream of music into our home. He is content with either an adult singing his favorite song, him serenading you, or just having music playing on the stereo. While Peyton has had difficulty attending to sounds, he seems to process music extremely well. We believe that Peyton's love of music has helped bring along the expansion of his expressive speech. He may not be able to spontaneously create many sentences yet, but he can sing an entire song. It is a rote form of learning. However, we have gained improvements in his language by "forgetting" lines that Peyton now readily fills in. He first started saying "No" using this method. His ability to make choices has greatly expanded. It's amazing how many verses there can be for "Wheels on the Bus" when there needs to be. Now he even tries to create his own songs. Also, we have watched Peyton's interest in symbolic play dramatically increase when partnered with music.

THE BEGINNING

I think many of us feel that there have been a few moments that totally changed the course of our lives — whether by happenstance or by a purposeful choice. For Peyton, his life seemed to start out on a course that only became more treacherous as we moved forward. It has taken several very serious turns, and a few detours, to get us back on a road that seems much more promising.

After an uneventful pregnancy, we had a scare during delivery. Peyton's heart rate would drop with each push as the umbilical cord was wrapped around his neck. After all the worry about his heart rate, the delivery room was full with a crew of at least twelve present at his birth. This was our first opportunity to see people rally when a little person is in trouble. As soon as he was born, he was whisked over to a team of intensive care nurses who checked him over. The news was good. We thought we had dodged a bullet, and nothing more terrible would happen.

After five months of colic, Peyton finally reached a period of two blissful months. We expected everything was going to get better from here. He was giggling, sitting on his own and transferring objects with his hands. The only real worry we had was that he was not babbling yet.

THE ONSET OF SEIZURES

Just before turning eight months, the seizures began. At first, it just appeared to be some quirky movements. Something any baby could do, right? Unfortunately, they were becoming too consistent and in clusters. I knew in my heart something was wrong. When we took him for his first electroenchephalogram (EEG), a study of his brain waves, we learned that these jerky movements were indeed seizures and a very serious form of epilepsy called infantile spasms. I'll never forget the discussion I had with Peyton's pediatrician about the diagnosis. I asked her if this was a fatal type of illness. Her reply was that it would not be life threatening, but life altering.

This was the point when my husband and I could choose two courses of action: (1) denial — become so absorbed with the grief of the situation that we did nothing, or (2) action — be proactive since every day is critical. Fortunately, we are both stubborn and determined people, so the choice was easy to get moving. We also had family members there to help us. If not for them, we could never have progressed forward from that point with as much energy and confidence.

Faced with a child with significant needs, we learned two very critical points. First, you quickly realize that you are your child's only, and therefore, best advocate. Only you have the responsibility to locate the doctors and therapists, rally them to your cause, and continue to help spread vital pieces of communication among the team members. Second, if you didn't realize it before, you and your significant other are a team. As teammates, you both must come to the understanding that there is a much better chance for things to progress smoothly if you work and laugh together. There is no way that Peyton could have done so well without this teamwork and the constant support from family.

During the next year, we were consumed with determining the extent of the epilepsy, and more importantly how to stop it. On a given day, he could have as many as a hundred seizures when he would drop his head down and raise both arms up toward his head. It was so difficult to watch and wait for these repetitive movements to subside. There would also be periods of staring episodes where you felt completely helpless in trying to reach him.

This form of seizure activity was considered generalized, which meant the electrical bursts of energy jolted throughout his entire brain. Instead of keeping track of all his developmental firsts, we tracked the frequency and severity of these daily seizure clusters. The seizures were preventing Peyton from acquiring many new skills. We were so afraid of how he would ever have the chance to develop normally with these constant seizures. Fortunately, there is an excellent comprehensive epilepsy center at our local hospital, Strong Memorial Hospital in Rochester, New York. Our neurologist, Dr. Giuseppe Erba, had the patience and experience to keep pushing ahead, at our persistent pace, with new attempts to stop the seizures. (Since then, he has been a wonderful resource in our constant vigilance over Peyton's progress.)

There turned out to be many different tests for Peyton to go through to determine the extent of the problem. During this investigatory phase, he had four magnetic resonance imaging tests (MRI), four other forms of brain imagings, about twenty blood tests, a spinal tap, and seven individual EEG monitorings (with an additional five since then). Then there was a weeklong EEG session to fully appreciate the actual source of the seizures. This meant keeping Peyton in a hospital crib while his head was covered with twenty-five electrodes, all pulled together in one big cord, attached to a computer system.

All along the way, these procedures were incredibly draining for all of us. Even with sedation, Peyton would become extremely upset. It was scary for him and us. How could you ever reassure a toddler that it will be okay going in that long narrow MRI tube for forty-five minutes, or having twenty-five EEG electrodes glued to his head? I can't even begin to explain the guilt that accompanies the act of physically restraining your screaming child on a table so that a procedure can be completed. All the while, we kept our eyes on the ultimate goal, discovering what was wrong inside of that precious little head.

Besides all the procedures, we tried six different medications, including one that we injected with a needle into his thigh up to three times a day. This medication turned our nine-month-old baby into a twenty-nine pound little sumo wrestler who preferred to sit and watch life go by. Since none of the medicines seemed to work, we turned to a recommended alternative diet as a solution.

The ketogenic diet involved exact measurements of food that could only be served to him if it was smothered in as much fat (butter or mayo) as possible. This strategy offered only partial help. The seizures persisted and developmental milestones continued to be missed.

The Internet was a wonderful source of information for us. My husband found a chat group where we communicated with people worldwide who were at different stages of the fight. We learned which drugs had the least side effects, what it was like for the child and family, who the best doctors were, among other things. Links to other sites contained additional details about his disorder. Our doctors were correct that we needed to maintain a clear perspective on our child's situation when reading descriptions about the illness. The prognosis was devastating enough, especially if you read the literature without understanding how your child's situation compared to the one being discussed.

The most important tip from the Internet was about a doctor in Detroit who specialized in this form of epilepsy. Dr. Harry Chugani couldn't have been more helpful. He was completely confident about where the problem areas were in Peyton's brain. He explained that surgery was Peyton's last hope to stop this terrible intractable form of epilepsy. At least we had the surgical option, since only about fifteen percent of the children with this disorder do. On the other hand, there were no guarantees that the surgery would stop the seizures, and there were very significant risks, including death. However, nothing had worked to stop the seizures and the quality of Peyton's life looked very bleak if we remained with the status quo.

We decided to go ahead with the surgery at Strong Hospital, with Dr. Webster Pilcher, a respected neurosurgeon who participated in the entire process, not just at the time of surgery. It was important to us to have regular access to the surgeon, not only during the hospital stay, but for the next year and longer.

THE LAST RESORT: BRAIN SURGERY

At nineteen months, Peyton underwent a partial hemispherectomy to resect two focal lesions on the left side of his brain that were causing the seizure activity. The process included two craniotomies a week apart. The first surgery included removing a portion of Peyton's skull to insert a grid of electrodes that provided a map delineating the source of the seizures. These more precise EEG results showed that the true impact of the seizures was far greater than we had originally realized. They also tried to determine where the motor and sensory strips in his brain were located. They wanted to leave these strips untouched to prevent paralysis. This was not an exact science because Peyton could not explain what he felt during the testing. We needed to accept that leaps of faith must be taken even in this arena where technology continues to evolve.

The second surgery involved once again opening Peyton's skull to remove the electrode grid and the brain tissue causing the seizures. The resection removed almost the entire temporal, parietal, and occipital lobes, as well as the hippocampus on the left side of his brain. This extraction represented about a quarter of Peyton's cortical tissue.

It was an agonizing two weeks living at the hospital. We tried to make Peyton comfortable, but he could not explain what he was feeling or the degree of pain he was in. Our pediatrician endearingly called him "little staplehead," because he had about thirty staples covering the two scars that ran across the middle and down the side of his head. It was ultimately Peyton's incredible spirit that pulled him through this crisis.

The result of the surgery was twofold. First, for the first time in a year, there was NO visible seizure activity! Second, he was left with significant developmental delays due to the twelve months of seizure activity, and from the brain tissue that was never useful to him. The major functional areas that were compromised included: (1) receptive language and links to expressive speech, (2) auditory processing and memory retention, (3) visual processing/perception/right vision field cut, (4) motor planning/body positioning, and (5) sensation/touch for specific fine motor skills.

The next step was remediation. Not only would we have to help him to rewire his brain, but also to recreate several processing centers that were removed. For us, that old adage that you only use ten percent of your brain took on a new perspective. Fortunately, scientists have discovered that the brain is indeed rather plastic. With deliberate stimulation, the brain is capable of rewiring itself, so that certain functions normally completed by one area can be redeveloped by another. This can take time, and is reliant on the strength of the remaining brain tissue, which in Peyton's case was not without its faults either.

Fortunately, Peyton did not regress during his battle with the seizures. Children frequently do with this form of epilepsy. However, he gained only a few new skills. Once the seizures stopped, he learned to walk at twenty-one months. Peyton's personality was finally starting to emerge. Yet his communication and motor planning skills were extremely limited. He had no words or signs by his two-year well visit to the pediatrician's office. A speech evaluation indicated that his expressive language skills were that of a four month old. Once again, we were extremely fearful of what we would hear next.

THE DEVELOPMENTAL DIAGNOSIS

When Peyton was two years old, Dr. Susan Hyman, a developmental pediatrician at Strong Hospital gave us the discouraging news. She diagnosed Peyton as falling within the autism spectrum, primarily because of "his lack of facial expression, diminished eye gaze to regulate social interaction, and lack of communicative intent." It remains unclear whether Peyton was destined to have autism or if the underlying brain insult presented an atypical etiology of his autistic behaviors. It is incredible to note that the National Alliance for Autism Research (NAAR) states that autism spectrum disorders occur in an estimated one in every 250 births. Some studies place the prevalence of autism spectrum disorders even higher.

At this point, Peyton had global developmental delays in language, cognition, motor, social, and adaptive skills that were greater than thirty-three percent. The complicating factor was that the resected parts of Peyton's brain controlled several key components involved in the learning process. We would need to help him rebuild these areas, and then utilize them to begin acquiring the missing skills. The extent of these issues emphasized that we needed to find an extremely qualified team of doctors and therapists to develop an individualized strategy that utilized Peyton's strengths to help him overcome his many challenges.

Having finally succeeded on the medical front, we had no idea that a much more complicated and anxious road lay ahead. During the year working with the medical team, there appeared to be no black and white choices. In the developmental arena, there are so many choices of methods to use and providers to choose from. Many of the options are considered to be experimental. So, not only do you have to be concerned about the impact on your child, but you may also be expected to pay for the services without assistance from your insurance carrier. Then, it is not always clear if a particular methodology is working, so a high level of patience is necessary. Finally, I have learned that you need to remain confident in your abilities to navigate through these relatively uncharted waters. Each child's set of challenges is so different that the selection and combination of services you decide upon will likewise be unique.

DESIGNING AN INTENSIVE
THERAPEUTIC PROGRAM

Dr. Hyman recommended that we consider two developmental models for delivering the therapy to Peyton. The first, better known for children with autism, is applied behavioral analysis (ABA), and was suggested because of the documented research supporting its benefit. Dr. O. Ivar Lovaas is credited with constructing this approach. ABA is a highly structured method that uses techniques of reinforcement to teach new behavioral and cognitive skills. You work with a consultant, usually a psychologist, who helps you create a number of programs that target specific skill acquisition. The therapists that implement these strategies use reinforcers (e.g., food or toys) and keep tabulated records of the child's progress. The risk with ABA is that you may create a little robot who cannot generalize the skills he learns.

The other methodology is called the developmental, individual differences, and relationship-based (DIR) model. This approach was created by Dr. Stanley Greenspan and Dr. Serena Wieder and is discussed in their book, *The Child with Special Needs: Encouraging Intellectual and Emotional Growth*. Dr. Stanley Greenspan is Clinical Professor of Psychiatry, Behavioral Science, and Pediatrics at George Washington University Medical Center, a practicing child psychiatrist, and the author of several books regarding child development. Dr. Serena Wieder is a clinical psychologist in private practice, specializing in the diagnosis and treatment of infants and young children. We have had the good fortune to work with both of these extraordinary people on Peyton's developmental issues.

The DIR model focuses on the individual strengths and needs of the child when planning the educational goals. The social/emotional goals are at the forefront of this process. The thinking is that if you increase the child's affect in a given situation, his social reciprocity will also rise, and you can begin to close more "circles of communication." An integral part of this model is something called "Floor Time," developed by Dr. Greenspan. It supports letting the child take the lead in play at his level and encouraging choice making and a spontaneous flow of communication. By treating everything your child does as intentional and purposeful, you will help increase his confidence level. While we have used this method more on an unstructured basis, it can easily be adapted when more structure is required.

We felt that DIR was the more appropriate method to focus on. While Peyton wanted to interact with others, he did not know how to initiate or to maintain a sequence of exchanges. We needed to start with the basics of social reciprocity — attention and mutual engagement, to build up to a two-way flow of communication. The next steps would then involve Peyton developing and expressing his ideas, and then connecting them in a logical way.

To find out more about this approach, I attended several conferences organized by Dr. Greenspan and Dr. Wieder through the Interdisciplinary Council on Developmental and Learning Disorders (ICDL). These seminars are designed for both professionals and parents. You come away with many new ideas and a renewed sense of invigoration having heard of the potential progress a child can make.

At our first visit with Dr. Greenspan, when Peyton was 2, he provided further vital diagnostic information. He explained that

Peyton's primary challenges stemmed from significant motor planning problems. The connections in his brain responsible for oral, gross, and fine motor skills were not working properly. While his symptom profile has many traits of autism, he is warm and engaging and tries to connect with others.

Dr. Greenspan outlined a thorough intensive therapeutic program. Within two months we had established a program that included twenty-five hours of therapy time (more than tripling the prior allotment). His weekly schedule included time at home, and at various clinics where we could take advantage of the therapists' equipment. We designed an intensive program that included DIR and ABA intervention, speech therapy, occupational therapy, physical therapy, and a music therapy. We also supplemented these therapies with a sensory integration program and additional play groups. We relied on two teams, each consisting of a psychologist and special educator, to implement the DIR and ABA components. We used some ABA to directly target certain cognitive skills. However, we modified this very strict approach and used the method for its specifically designed programs and track sheets. We use neither the intense style of delivery nor reinforcers. Finally, my husband and I needed to use the Floor Time method of play with Peyton as often as possible.

THE IMPACTS OF AN INTENSIVE SCHEDULE

This significant increase in his weekly routine of therapy came at a good time. Peyton had had a year to recover from his surgery. He was now up for the challenge and seemed to have very few problems with the level of demands placed on him. While we understood the importance of having access to the therapy, we continually worried about the strain this busy schedule had on Peyton. A neurotypical child has so much more freedom to learn and to explore his environment. Fortunately, our therapists were very creative and made it enjoyable for him to participate in the learning process. Peyton's weekly schedule included therapy daily, from breakfast until dinner. A typical day was comprised of having therapists either coming into our home or driving him to appointments elsewhere. There were many days when we would have at least five different people come and go at our house. It can be a bit of a juggling act, and can lead to a high level of stress. I continue to struggle about how to incorporate the many helpful suggestions we receive.

In the past few years, we have continued to make changes to his therapy program in terms of the number of hours per discipline and the people with whom he works. As Peyton continues to evolve, so must his program to keep challenging him forward. He is currently involved with a thirty-three-hour-per-week regimen of services that also includes five half-days of preschool. The social opportunities through school are very important in helping him learn to engage with his peers. Peyton has spent so much time with adults that try to understand and to elicit his communicative attempts that it is more difficult for Peyton to sustain an interaction with a peer.

We have added support for Assistive Technology, a therapy that uses technology to help a child acquire primarily language and fine motor skills. Many of the devices use the Picture Exchange Communication System (PECS), and act as a tireless teacher to foster communication or to provide an alternative to writing. This is a fascinating area where technology helps to open many more doors for your child.

We ensure that part of his week involves the necessary sensory components. Especially for kids with pervasive developmental disorder (PDD), the sensory issues can be an underlying factor for many motor planning, communication, cognitive, and mutual engagement issues. We have developed a sensory routine for him that includes a brushing protocol and joint compressions. He often wears a weighted vest or uses a t-stool to help him to pay attention. The sensory integration therapy, especially the vestibular and proprioceptive experiences, has proven to be vital in helping to rewire his brain.

To provide better examples of Peyton's developmental progress, I have asked one of our special educators and one of our speech pathologists to share their own experiences with Peyton. Both of these women have worked with Peyton for almost three years, so they know him very well.

From Signa Trowbridge, a Special Educator:

I remember the first time meeting Peyton's team of professionals. I knew I was beginning a journey. After a week of visiting Peyton, I realized that the smallest interaction I could get from him was a monumental step. The clinical psychologist, who was directing the ABA portion of his program, and I constantly adjusted our direction and goals to match more closely where Peyton was at any given time. Work was consistently based on incremental steps toward interaction and engagement. We soon learned that to accomplish any ABA work, we needed to recognize Peyton's intentions and desires, and acknowledge those with persistence and perseverance. The first year of work was this type of recognition and concentration.

As we began our second year together, Peyton's program continued to be refined. With Peyton's desires and intentions still at the forefront, I was able to reach him a bit more each day. Table work increased to five to ten minutes twice each session, with heavy emphasis on his interests. Stress about any structured table work still prevailed but his recovery time from this stress was lessened. Communication was basic sign and single words. Petyon was hard to understand, but at least he was giving effort in the language area. By the end of this second year, comments on past service notes included "great interactive day," "beginning to point appropriately," "expressively labeling objects with single words," and "initiated table work." What a difference!

The third year of my work has seen a boy blossom in engagement, pretend play, communication, attention, and work habits. He now very often initiates table work because he is becoming confident and proud of the work he produces. Identifying letters in his name as well as others, cutting independently with scissors, speaking in seven-word sentences, emerging in back and forth conversations with appropriately answering questions, building structures of tunnels and bridges as he engages in toy play, acting out characters such as a train engineer, a bus driver, and a basketball player are just a few of the skills developed. He sustains engagement for the full hour and a half I spend with him including initiating and following through with thirty-five to fifty minutes of table work and play. Unbelievable progress, unbelievable development, and an unbelievable kid!

From Joyce Porzi, a Speech Pathologist:

Peyton first received speech therapy services at twenty-five months of age. At that time, his vocalizations were limited to "ah" and signing consisted of manipulating the therapist's hands to form "more." Peyton enjoyed sensory-motor games like tickling and chasing, exhibiting joint attention and engagement for these activities.

About six months later, Peyton had improved his joint attention for favorite activities like ball play, bubbles, and songs. Nonverbal circles of communication were increasing and Peyton was beginning to make choices for songs using gestures/signs and photos. Oral sensory stimulation tasks were not tolerated well. At thirty-one months, Peyton spoke his first word. While having a snack in the kitchen, he requested "more" by pronoucing "maw." This was truly a "precious moment."

When Peyton was thirty-seven months, PECS was introduced and proved successful for increasing intentional sign and verbal communication. Over time, Peyton has received speech therapies in both the classroom and at home. So many wonderful and skilled professionals and family members have contributed to Peyton's program, reinforcing communication goals, which accounts for the marvelous gains he has made.

Currently Peyton is a five year old, transitioning to the school-aged population. He communicates primarily with spoken words, in sentences of up to eight words in length. Verbal turn taking is increasing, giving adults the pleasure of "conversing" with Peyton. His speech intelligibility has improved dramatically through a combination of traditional articulation therapy, sound and syllable sequence drills, and intensive oral sensory-motor work. Peyton now tolerates about fifteen to twenty minutes of muscle stretches, blowing, sucking, and oral imitation tasks daily. He is better able to imitate lip movements, while his tongue remains weak and in need of continued exercise.

AIT has had a tremendous impact on Peyton's speech and language development. This intervention has been instrumental in improving Peyton's attention to sound and spoken language, giving him the ability to make better use of verbal models for the acquisition of speech sounds as well as for ongoing receptive language skill development.

Even though Peyton's attentional and ongoing neurological issues still can negatively impact his performance, he has been to me a shining example of persistence and success in the face of monumental hurdles. Knowing this amazing little boy has been a privilege and tremendous learning experience for me.

THE AUDIOLOGICAL COMPONENT

Dr. Greenspan has dramatically helped us by referring other specialists who have been able to provide additional consultative services. His first recommendation was for us to see Dr. Jane Madell for an audiological evaluation. He indicated that Peyton might be a candidate for auditory integration training (AIT). AIT is a therapy in which listening to altered music through earphones is done in a systematic fashion in an effort to alter the central neurophysiology. The decision to visit Dr. Madell and use AIT turned out to be extremely important. Next to the surgery, this intervention has had the greatest impact on his development.

Dr. Madell is a trained audiologist and speech pathologist with over thirty years of experience. She is currently the Director of the Hearing and Learning Center at Beth Israel Hospital in New York City. We prefer going to Dr. Madell for several reasons. Her reputation is excellent in this field. She is very persistent during the evaluations and is direct with her opinions. A primary aspect of her practice is the delivery of AIT, having trained extensively with Dr. Bérard, who developed the AIT program in France. She has received approval to complete a much needed study to demonstrate the benefits of AIT.

Her clinic has a broad array of audiological equipment. One of the criticisms of AIT is that many of the people who do it are not properly trained or don't have the appropriate technology. We feel very confident in Dr. Madell's abilities.

We had two hearing tests for Peyton when he was younger, and they indicated his hearing was "fine." After our first visit with Dr. Madell (Peyton was 3), we learned that hearing is only the first step. Obviously, the more you hear, the greater the input into your brain. While our local audiologists were content to confirm hearing out of only one ear, Dr. Madell persisted to confirm Peyton can hear from both ears. (A true miracle given his brain surgery.) Once the degree of hearing is confirmed, it is the person's ability to process and attend to the sounds that dictates the interpretation and use of what is heard. Her diagnosis was that Peyton had severe auditory processing and attention issues, as he was very hyposensitive to sounds. It was almost like he was deaf in that he was processing only a small percentage of what he could actually hear. His language would improve at a very slow rate until we adequately addressed these issues. With this diagnosis, she recommended strongly that Peyton undergo a round of AIT.

We felt like there must have been divine intervention at this

point, because just that morning of our appointment, a rare cancellation occurred. We could stay on for the next two weeks to
proceed with the AIT, instead of waiting another six months for
an available appointment. It was a difficult time since I was eight
months pregnant with my second child. We thought we would be
in New York City for a day, not two weeks.

During the first week of the AIT, we spent four hours each
day commuting back and forth in Manhattan traffic to Dr.
Madell's office. All of the inconvenience was worth it. I really can't
convey to you the transformation in Peyton's attention even after
the first week. All of a sudden, he was able to follow simple one-
step directions. He was responding much better to his name. He
was trying a few more signs. We were ecstatic. However, this was
just the beginning in his recovery. Peyton's auditory attention
problem was so severe that Dr. Madell cautioned us that in these
cases, we would most likely need to do several rounds of AIT. The
hope was that his brain would continue to make the necessary
improvements of processing auditory input, and disseminating the
information properly.

THE IMPACT OF AIT

Over the past two years since we began our relationship with Dr.
Madell, we spent a total of two months in New York City completing four rounds of AIT. After each time, there has been an
amazing change in Peyton's language. It is not just the family who
witnesses the results. The entire therapy team has been in awe of
what the AIT has done for Peyton's communication abilities. The
increase in his language skills has set off a ripple effect that has
begun to help him in all his other areas of work.

After the second round of AIT, we continued to see dramatic
improvements in his receptive language. He was starting to initiate

more, albeit still using a combination of words, signs, and gestures. He noticed many more sounds in his environment, like unfamiliar voices, and airplanes in the sky. He was finally emerging from his "cocoon," and beginning to appreciate and to discern the sounds in the world around him.

It was after the third round that I think he made the greatest leap with his language skills. At the age of four, Peyton finally started to imitate words and sounds. His expressive speech dramatically took off. He was finally able to start practicing verbally with words. This may sound strange, but Peyton never babbled and even as his speech progressed, it was always sporadic. This step was huge. The fourth round brought more positive gains. His speech intelligibility improved. His speech therapist was able to proceed with a formal articulation program, something she was never sure she would do with Peyton. He also began to string more words together into phrases. Just recently, we have been able to have brief conversations with him.

The spikes in his rate of language acquisition have occurred only after each AIT session. We have been careful to note any other changes in his developmental program that could help account for these dramatic improvements. There were none. We can't adequately explain it, but the AIT must be responsible. While the brain surgery was critical in allowing Peyton to develop at all, the AIT has given him the chance to learn by properly processing the sounds around him.

The exciting aspect of AIT is that it *can* change the way an individual will perceive sound. It helps with the central auditory processing capabilities of the brain. In other words, a person may be able to attend more thoroughly to the world around him because the brain has better adapted itself to accept and to process incoming sounds. As a parent, I can't help think that other children with seizure disorders might also benefit from AIT. Epilepsy can affect any part of the brain, yet a relatively high percentage of epilepsy stems from abnormalities in the left temporal lobe. It is also within the left temporal lobe that auditory processing is typically handled. It would be very interesting to understand the degree to which these aspects are linked.

OTHER DEVELOPMENTAL INTERVENTIONS

Along the way, we have worked with several other developmental specialists who have each had a dramatic impact on Peyton's advancement. Of course, networking for new contacts and ideas is a never-ending process. Quite often, one relationship has then led to another.

Given the complexity of Peyton's case, we have had to rely on many people because each one tends to focus on only part of the problem. In certain fields, we also have to find people that think about the entire processing loop. We have learned that for Peyton, it is not necessarily his body parts that don't work. It's the connections within his brain that don't allow those parts to function properly. The following discussion involves some of the specialists who have provided additional assistance in helping to strengthen these connections.

SYMBOLIC PLAY AND LANGUAGE DEVELOPMENT

Dr. Serena Wieder has given us many useful suggestions on how to help Peyton with his symbolic play using the DIR method. His motor planning challenges make it very difficult for him to sequence together even a few steps during his play. Peyton learns best when the individual steps can be broken down for him. The ability to imitate does not come easily for him. We have incorporated many of her ideas into our own floor time sessions with

Peyton. Also, our music therapist has worked on some of Dr. Wieder's recommendations, since Peyton is so motivated by music. The music therapist utilizes her DIR training "to develop expressive freedom, communication, and interresponsiveness." "When music and singing activities are involved, whether it be composed music, instrumental activities, songs about specific topics, or songs for learning, Peyton remains involved, interested, less frustrated, and less withdrawn." She utilizes his high affect to encourage him to respond to the rhythm or to act out the scenarios in a song. "Due to the nature of Peyton's medical history, music is essential in that it is processed in all areas of the brain and may be instrumental in aiding in the process of redeveloping strengths and the acquisition of new behaviors and skills in the remaining portions of his brain." This form of therapy has resulted in nice gains with his overall language development, imitation skills, and pretend play.

It was also Dr. Wieder that first told us that Peyton's verbal ability would eventually be one of his strengths. This comment seemed so strange to us at the time, because he was still relying on his signs and PECS cards for his communication. We were still not clear that words would be his primary source of language. But she was right! We couldn't wait for him to start talking, and now it doesn't seem like he can be quiet! He talks all day long, expressing his needs and singing songs. Our primary focus now is on expanding his spontaneous use of words and sequencing them together.

SPEECH

Dr. Greenspan suggested a consultation with Diane Lewis, a speech pathologist in his area with expertise in oral motor therapy. During our consultations, she provided many great ideas on how to improve Peyton's oral motor planning issues. We took these sug-

gestions home and our speech pathologist has been able to incorporate them into Peyton's therapy with noticeable gains.

Dr. Greenspan and Ms. Lewis have collaborated on a therapy
protocol they call The Affect-Based Language Curriculum
(ABLC): An Intensive Program for Families. It is an innovative
approach to the development of language that uses the benefits of
the DIR model. The curriculum uses systematic instruction with
applied Floor Time to work on advancing a child's development of
receptive and expressive language, imitation, pragmatics, and
engagement. Additional strategies are discussed involving oral
motor and augmentative communication techniques. Included in
the manual are worksheets to determine the level of your child's
language skills across several different areas. These worksheets help
you to plan goals and objectives, and to discover the inconsisten-
cies in his skill acquisition. Our speech pathologist is using this
information to refine her approach to his therapy time and to
enhance his language development.

VISION

Dr. Madell referred us to an optometrist in Morristown, New
Jersey, who specializes in vision therapy. Dr. Marianne Cidis discovered that Peyton was significantly farsighted. This was a difficult diagnosis to make since, at the time, Peyton could not provide
any verbal input to assist with the evaluation. With the introduction of glasses, his attention to tasks improved, as did his eye contact. To help him overcome his vision field loss, we tried prism
lenses for a short period but did not find them helpful in his case.
She also provided a few activities to help improve his use of vision.

Just recently we visited Dr. Harry Wachs, an optometrist
with over forty-five years of experience. He is the director of the
Vision and Conceptual Development Center (VCDC) in

Washington, D.C. Dr. Wachs believes that, "Vision involves utilizing knowledge acquired through visual experience. Efficient and well-developed vision results in understanding what one sees and coordinating that knowledge with one's body." After his evaluation, he alerted us to the fact that Peyton lacks certain "schemes" (or sequencing skills) usually acquired between three and six months of age. He will continue to have difficulty with many fine motor tasks until he masters the schemes he lacks. We plan to return to the VCDC every month for three days to learn which activities will help Peyton strengthen his visual processing capabilities. We expect that they will also help Peyton with his binocular coordination, tracking, convergence, focusing, fusion flexibility and stamina, and depth perception abilities.

ATTENTION

Currently, we are considering options that we hope will help to optimize Peyton's attention level. We feel that this is an ongoing problem that is compromising both his academic performance and his ability to participate in social activities. If something is motivating to him, he will sit for many minutes and participate. However, on average, his attention span is very short, less than five minutes. During testing periods, his inattention to task resulted in findings that were below his true skill level.

Besides changing the anticonvulsant medication he uses, we are receiving consultative services from Kelly Dorfman, a nutritionist in the Washington, D.C., area. Ms. Dorfman has an excellent reputation working with children who have PDD, and was referred to us by Dr. Serena Wieder. She uses several different approaches to maximize the child's nutritional intake. She recommended that we provide Peyton with additional essential and structured fats to help strengthen the connections within his brain.

A specially formulated vitamin will insure that Peyton has the proper nutrients in his diet.

THE ROLE AS PEYTON'S ADVOCATE

There are times when no matter how well-intentioned the professional, you know that this person either doesn't possess the appropriate skill set, or doesn't have the right demeanor to work with your child. It's difficult to go back and find someone new, but it's worse to waste time and remain frustrated. Our experiences of having to replace certain professionals on the team occurred early on; so I learned the importance of thoroughly explaining Peyton's issues and stressing our requirements when trying to find the right providers. These mild setbacks were always quickly resolved and resulted in positive gains.

The most upsetting experience came when we hired a psychologist for a one-time evaluation. Unfortunately, we did not appreciate his limited ability to deal with complex cases until it was too late. In completing his evaluation, he spent less than an hour with Peyton, and proclaimed him mentally retarded. This news was surprising and devastating. Fortunately, I did not have to struggle with this for long because the overall consensus from our intervention team was that this diagnosis was totally inappropriate given Peyton's medical history and continued progress. I further learned that the diagnosis of mental retardation should only be considered when a child, enrolled in an optimal program, no longer makes any progress for a period of two years. Peyton's progress has never plateaued since the surgery.

We don't know what the future will hold for Peyton. As a parent of a child with special needs, you need to rely on the expertise of the professionals who evaluate your child. You make very important decisions based on those recommendations. A diagnosis, in particular, can have very serious ramifications. This was a difficult lesson to learn.

As Peyton's advocate, I have had to rely on many of my professional skills. Our work with Peyton's school district's Committee on Special Education has required a high level of organizational, negotiating, and marketing skills. We have truly appreciated the collaborative efforts with the school administrators that have allowed us to establish the most appropriate educational plan for Peyton. They have allowed me to select the best therapists in our area within each discipline, even though this meant that they came from several different agencies.

Each year when I see the several inch stack of papers that is Peyton's Individualized Education Program (IEP), I am astounded. To help summarize the important aspects and to make sure our thoughts are highlighted, I produce an annual brochure about Peyton, with his picture prominently displayed on the front. The creation of these documents allows me to focus on the big picture and how all the various components come together. I also use them as a way to quickly communicate what we are pursuing for him with the rest of his intervention team.

A MOM'S POINT OF VIEW

Along this journey, I have definitely learned many things about myself. My greatest struggle continues to be dealing with the guilt that somehow I caused his illness. As soon as you become pregnant, you are constantly reminded that the life developing inside of you relies on you. I worked so hard to do everything my doctor told me to ensure the safest environment for him. Yet something went wrong, as it does in two percent of all births. How can you then step back and not accept responsibility for what your child must suffer through? My family and doctors all have told me that there was nothing I could have done and not to blame myself. It could be that I am just somehow trying to take control for a situation where there is no answer.

It is the sense of urgency and my guilt that provide that spark inside me to keep pushing. To keep plugging along with all that needs to be done for Peyton. I may have heard the term "special needs" only a few times before Peyton was born. Now it is a daily concern. I also learned that in another strange twist of fate, Peyton's battle has provided many blessings I never would have experienced. We truly appreciate so many more moments of his development since they usually come with so much work. We've learned how truly horrible and miraculous the brain can be by creating seizures and then by helping to repair itself. Moreover, we have met such amazing doctors, therapists, and administrators, and have witnessed how hard they try to help our son.

A NOTE ABOUT AIT AND A TODDLER

Our younger son, Ryan, has cruised through the majority of developmental milestones for his age. It has been a wonderful experience to see how a child just innately acquires skills. It's also been a pleasure to see how Ryan worships his older brother. They learned early on that you can have fun together with only gestures and giggles.

The one area of concern we have had with Ryan is his expressive language. He was late to babble, about seven months, and has had limited production of sounds and words. While he said a handful of words around his first birthday, we only heard them a few times and then not again. Ryan would sometimes act as if he didn't even hear you. At other times he would respond very quickly. His receptive language was evaluated as right on track, and socially he was slightly ahead. To be honest, if we did not have the experiences with Peyton, we most likely would have waited until his second birthday to get a speech evaluation.

However, it was difficult not to be hypervigilant about Ryan's development. We asked Peyton's speech therapist to evaluate Ryan at fifteen months. Sure enough, she discovered several red flags that made her concerned that Ryan may have a form of oral dyspraxia.

- Better receptive skills as compared with expressive language skills.
- Silent "posturing" of the mouth when attempting speech imitation.
- Delayed sound imitation and sound play. Babbling started later than typical and was limited in occurrence and in variety of sounds used.
- Sound repertoire restricted to 2–3 vowels and 2–3 consonants. (He would label most things as "dee.")
- Nonspeech sounds (i.e., car noises, animal sounds) also occurred later than typical.
- Ryan could spontaneously produce a complex word like "biscuit" clearly, but had difficulty with a word like "mama."
- Attempts at nonspeech oral imitation (i.e., blowing and puckering) were difficult and unsuccessful.

Her assessment also showed that Ryan had evidence of weakness in the oral area. He displayed an open mouth posture with some drooling. This was often accompanied with his tongue protruding. Late teeth eruption (at thirteen months) and a significant underbite resulted in him often letting his tongue rest on his lips. He had a weak lip seal on horns and reduced lip rounding. While he took well to a straw cup after weaning off the bottle, he would often suckle versus suck on the straw. Finally, she had concerns for auditory processing because he was highly inconsistent in responding to his name or known environmental sounds. Most people who meet Ryan agree he is a very bright and happy child, but a very visual learner.

We explained our concerns to Dr. Madell when seeing her for a follow-up appointment with Peyton. We had taken Ryan to two local audiologists, but could not obtain a diagnosis. They both told us that Ryan was too young and not testable. We told Dr. Madell that, and she laughed, explaining that no child is untestable, but rather the audiologist can't test the child. She completed a visual reinforcement audiometry test with Ryan. During the test, I held Ryan on my lap in the soundproof room. It was agony. I would hear a sound, but Ryan would just not respond to it for many seconds longer than appropriate. Dr. Madell's diagnosis for Ryan was very poor auditory attention. She explained that even at Ryan's age (nineteen months), he would benefit from AIT.

We were always amazed at the improvement in Peyton's expressive and receptive language following the training. But, there were several medical reasons for Peyton to complete AIT. We were not sure what to expect with Ryan. Fortunately, he had very little difficulty getting through the training. Once again, we began to see dramatic changes in Ryan's expressive language attempts.

After the first week of AIT, he imitated his first sound, a piggy squeal. Since then, he has tried imitating so many more words and sounds, animal and nonsense ones. His audiological exam after the two weeks of AIT showed marked improvements. This time, he immediately was turning to the sounds, and even to some I did not even hear! His speech pathologist was also impressed when we returned home. She remarked that he was sounding like a different child. In just three months following the AIT, Ryan's expressive vocabulary ballooned from five words to over fifty. Yet, we still feel that Ryan could benefit from additional AIT, as he continues to rely too heavily on his visual versus auditory skills.

Going through the AIT process has involved a significant time and financial commitment. The bottom line for us is that it has been extremely helpful. I don't even want to think about where Peyton or Ryan would be developmentally without it. Yet, our experiences with both boys show that this method can help children with very different developmental and medical histories. All you need is to find the right people to identify the problem and to complete the AIT.

CONCLUSION

To be honest, this story has been difficult to write. I have learned that it is a very emotional process for me to replay the first few years of Peyton's life without getting bogged down in the memories. For survival purposes, I focus on the short-term future, and what the next steps are for us. That has been my methodology when responding to his medical crisis, and while navigating through the developmental sea of options.

In Peyton's short life, he has had over *two hundred* doctor appointments and procedures. In total, he has spent a month in the hospital. His medical history is complicated, and it continues to be an issue. While we are light-years ahead of where we would have been without the surgery, Peyton's brain is still not fully cooperating with its owner. He has had five breakthrough seizures in the past year. He is still on anticonvulsant medication, although at a very low level. It's worrisome how long he will be on the medication and whether there will be any long-term effects.

As Peyton's advocate, I continue to seek out the best people to provide a unique intensive intervention strategy that employs multiple disciplines and a diverse set of therapy techniques. I have strived to convince the administrators who have the final determination over how many services he receives that he deserves an intensive therapeutic program and that he greatly benefits from it. All the effort to rally these people to help us has only emphasized the fact that I can't help Peyton recover by myself. As a parent, I think our first instincts are that it is up to us alone to solve the problems. However, when you have a child with special needs, it is not that easy. It takes a considerable amount of research and networking to uncover the facts necessary to support all the different decisions you are required to make in response to his illness and development. We have relied on a community of professionals to be open-minded and creative in their approaches. They have needed to adapt the protocols typically used with children that fall on the spectrum to fit Peyton's unique needs. While Peyton still has certain symptoms of autism, we hope that as his progress continues the appropriateness of that diagnosis will continue to decrease.

As in every child's life, there will surely be many happy times and disappointments to come as he grows into an adult. We have dreams for his future. It's just that we are really at the start of our journey together. There are still many unknowns. It would be great to have a crystal ball at this point to confirm my optimistic thoughts. Peyton's determination and willingness to work so hard have helped him make amazing progress in his efforts to gain new capabilities. He demonstrates time and again how his brain is miraculously rewiring itself. No matter what lies ahead, he will always be my hero for all that he has already lived through and triumphed over.

In closing, here is a poem I wrote for Peyton:

You hold your child's hand
and wonder what he feels.
You look into your child's eyes
and wonder what he sees.
You listen to your child's giggle,
and wonder what he thinks.
All are special moments, all are
integral to understanding the
miracles of development
— so often taken for granted.
You plan, you pray, and you wait.
You just know that someday it
will all become clear.
A hug,
a tear,
a smile,
a certainty.